The Politics of Risk Society

The
Politics
of Risk
Society

Edited by
Jane Franklin

Polity Press

PUBLISHED IN ASSOCIATION WITH THE
INSTITUTE FOR PUBLIC POLICY RESEARCH

Copyright © this collection Polity Press 1998
For further copyright details, please see the acknowledgements page.
First published in 1998 by Polity Press in association with Blackwell Publishers Ltd.
Transferred to digital print 2003

2 4 6 8 10 9 7 5 3 1

Editorial office:
Polity Press
65 Bridge Street
Cambridge CB2 1UR, UK

Marketing and production:
Blackwell Publishers Ltd
108 Cowley Road
Oxford OX4 1JF, UK

Published in the USA by
Blackwell Publishers Inc.
Commerce Place
350 Main Street
Malden, MA 02148, USA

ISBN 0-7456-1924-X
ISBN 0-7456-1925-8 (pbk)

A catalogue record for this book is available from the British Library.

Library of Congress Cataloging-in-Publication Data
The politics of risk society / edited by Jane Franklin.
     p.   cm.
     'The chapters of this volume are drawn from contributions to a
conference . . . organized by the Institute for Public Policy Research
in London in March 1996, and from a selection of articles and essays
which were published in journals and newspapers at the time'—Ack.
     'Published in association with the Institute for Public Policy
Research.'
     Includes bibliographical references and index.
     ISBN 0-7456-1924-X (hc : alk. paper). — ISBN 0-7456-1925-8 (pbk.
: alk. paper)
     1. Risk—Social aspects—Congresses. 2. Technology—Social
aspects—Congresses. 3. Policy sciences—Congresses. I. Franklin,
Jane. II. Institute for Public Policy Research (London, England)
HM201.P65 1998
303.44—dc21   97-29584
                                                                                    CIP

Typeset in 11 on 13 pt Sabon
by Graphicraft Typesetters Ltd., Hong Kong

Printed and bound in Great Britain by
Marston Lindsay Ross International Ltd,
Oxfordshire

Contents

Contributors   vii

Acknowledgements   xi

Introduction
Jane Franklin   1

1 Politics of Risk Society
  Ulrich Beck   9

2 Risk Society: the Context of British Politics
  Anthony Giddens   23

3 Lessons of Lloyd's: the Limits of Insurance
  Adam Raphael   35

4 Nature Bites Back
  John Gray   43

5 Risky Business, Safety
  Martin Woollacott   47

6 Risk Society, Politics and BSE
  Robin Grove-White   50

7 Procrastination, Precaution and the Global Gamble
  Stephen Tindale   54

8 Once the Men in White Coats Held the Promise
of a Better Future . . .
John Durant   70

9 There's Method in the Magic
Pat Kane   76

10 Technology and Democracy
Patricia Hewitt   83

11 People in Distress
Susie Orbach   90

12 Friendship: the Social Glue of Contemporary Society?
Ray Pahl   99

13 The Politics of Prevention
Martin Woollacott   120

14 Risk and Public Policy: Towards a High-Trust
Democracy
Anna Coote   124

Index   133

Contributors

Ulrich Beck is Professor of Sociology at the University of Munich and Distinguished Visiting Research Professor at the University of Wales in Cardiff. He is the author of *Risk Society: Towards a New Modernity* (Sage, 1992), *Ecological Politics in an Age of Risk* (Polity Press, 1995), *The Re-invention of Politics* (Polity Press, 1997) and *Democracy without Enemies* (Polity Press, 1998).

Anna Coote is Deputy Director of the Institute for Public Policy Research, where she initiated and now directs the Institute's work on Health and Social Policy, Media and Communications and Citizens' Juries. Her recent publications include *New Agenda for Health* with D. J. Hunter (IPPR, 1996), *Converging Communications* with C. Murroni and R. Collins (IPPR, 1996), and *Citizens' Juries* (IPPR, 1994).

John Durant is Assistant Director of the Science Museum and Professor of Public Understanding of Science at Imperial College, London. He is also Chairman of the European Federation of Biotechnology Task Group on Public Perceptions of Biotechnology, and a member of the UK Government's Advisory Committee on Genetic Testing. He is the founder editor of *Public Understanding of Science*, and in addition to academic publishing he writes and broadcasts regularly on scientific subjects for general audiences.

Jane Franklin is Research Fellow at the Institute for Public Policy Research. Her main research interest is in the relationship between social and political theory, politics and policy-making. She teaches on a course on Women and Politics at the University of North London and is editor of *Equality* (IPPR, 1997).

Anthony Giddens is Director of the London School of Economics. He has written widely in the field of sociology and social theory and contributes many articles and book reviews to professional journals, weeklies and newspapers. His most recent books include *The Transformation of Intimacy* (Polity Press, 1992), *Beyond Left and Right* (Polity Press, 1994) and, with Ulrich Beck and Scott Lash, *Reflexive Modernization* (Polity Press, 1994).

John Gray is Fellow of Jesus College, Oxford and Professor of Politics at Oxford University, and has been a visiting chair at Harvard and Yale universities. His recent publications include *Enlightenment's Wake* (Routledge, 1995); *Isaiah Berlin* (HarperCollins, 1996) and *Endgames* (Polity Press, 1997).

Robin Grove-White is Director of the Centre for the Study of Environmental Change (CSEC), Lancaster University. He is also a Forestry Commissioner, Chair of the Board of Greenpeace UK and a board member of the Green Alliance and Common Ground. He is a co-author of the recent report *Uncertain World: Genetically Modified Organisms, Food and Public Attitudes in Britain* (CSEC, 1997).

Patricia Hewitt is Member of Parliament for Leicester West. She is a trustee of the Institute for Public Policy Research and has written many books and reports, including *About Time: Revolution in Work and Family Life* (IPPR, 1993).

Pat Kane is a writer and musician. He contributes regularly to the *Guardian, New Statesman* and *Scotland on Sunday*, writes a weekly column for the *Herald* in Glasgow, and is currently editing *Blizzard*, an Internet music-and-culture magazine for Microsoft. He is also a lead singer with the Scottish jazz-soul band Hue & Cry.

Susie Orbach co-founded the Women's Therapy Centre in London in 1976, and in 1981 the Women's Therapy Centre Institute, a postgraduate training centre for psychotherapists in New York.

She has a practice seeing individuals and couples and supervising the work of other psychotherapists. Her books include *Hunger Strike: The Anorectic's Struggle as a Metaphor of our Age* (Penguin, 1986) and *What's Really Going On Here?* (Virago, 1994). She writes a column for the *Saturday Guardian* on emotional issues.

Ray Pahl is at the ESRC Research Centre on Micro-Social Change at the University of Essex, and Emeritus Professor of Sociology at the University of Kent at Canterbury since 1972. He is the author of many books and articles, including *Divisions of Labour* and *On Work* (both published by Blackwell) and, most recently, *After Success: Fin-de-Siècle Anxiety and Identity* (Polity Press, 1995).

Adam Raphael has been Home Affairs writer at *The Economist* since 1994. Previously, he was Political Editor of *The Observer*, and political correspondent and Washington correspondent of the *Guardian*. He is the author of *My Learned Friends* (W. H. Allen, 1990), *Grotesque Libels* (Corgi, 1993) and *Ultimate Risk: The Inside Story of the Lloyd's Catastrophe* (Bantam, 1994).

Stephen Tindale is Director of the Green Alliance and was, until recently, a Senior Research Fellow at the Institute for Public Policy Research. He is Lecturer in Environmental Politics at Birkbeck College, University of London and was previously Secretary to the Labour Party Policy Commission on the Environment. His recent publications include *The State of the Nations* (IPPR, 1996) and *Green Tax Reform* (IPPR, 1996) with Gerald Holtham.

Martin Woollacott is Foreign Affairs columnist of the *Guardian*. He was previously Foreign Editor, correspondent in the Middle East and correspondent in the Far East.

Acknowledgements

The chapters of this volume are drawn from contributions to a conference on the Politics of Risk Society, organized by the Institute for Public Policy Research in London in March 1996, and from a selection of articles and essays published at the time, which show how Ulrich Beck and Anthony Giddens's social analysis of risk resonates with real experience.

The editor would especially like to thank Anthony Giddens and Anna Coote for their help and support with the conference and with this book, and would also like to thank Ann Bone, Julia Harsant and Gill Motley of Polity Press.

Introduction © Jane Franklin; chapter 1 © Ulrich Beck; chapter 2 © Anthony Giddens; chapter 3 © Adam Raphael; chapter 4 by John Gray appeared previously in the *Guardian*, 26 March 1996 © The Guardian; chapter 5 by Martin Woollacott appeared previously in the *Guardian*, 28 March 1996 © The Guardian; chapter 6 appeared previously in the *Financial Times*, 29 March 1996 © Robin Grove-White; chapter 7 © Stephen Tindale; chapter 8 appeared previously in *The Independent*, 1 April 1996 © John Durant; chapter 9 by Pat Kane appeared previously in the *New Statesman*, 23 August 1996 © The New Statesman; chapter 10 © Patricia Hewitt; chapter 11 © Susie Orbach – extracts appeared originally in David Cannard and Neil Small (eds), *Living Together*, Quartet, 1997; chapter 12 © Ray Pahl; chapter 13 by Martin Woollacott appeared previously in the *Guardian*, 1 July 1995 © The Guardian; chapter 14 © Anna Coote.

Introduction

JANE FRANKLIN

Risk is not new. There has always been a contingent edge to life. What has changed is the *nature* of risk. This volume looks at risk in contemporary society, and illustrates how it is becoming a dynamic force for change in our individual and political lives. The way we interpret risk, negotiate risk, and live with the unforeseen consequences of modernity will structure our culture, society and politics for the coming decades.

The concept of risk society opens up individual and political opportunities. In contrast to postmodern despair, it presents an understanding of the internal and external dynamics of social change, which generate a realistic, yet hopeful, politics. The parameters of this theory are developed here by Ulrich Beck and Anthony Giddens. To understand risk society, they argue, we have to begin to think in a new way about the world we live in, to find a new language to describe what is happening to us. We have all become acutely aware of how it feels to live in risk society. It seems as though there is no way to negotiate the risks that now present themselves to us: global warming, BSE, the E-coli virus are beyond our control. We can't see them, we have no way of knowing if they are real, yet every day we have to decide whether or not to risk eating beef, risk drinking tap-water, risk going to our family butcher. We take these decisions in the light of conflicting information from experts and politicians, whom we can no longer trust to keep us informed.

The feeling this generates adds to our sense of insecurity, which embodies for Beck and Giddens the process of transition from one form of society to another: from the first phase to the second phase of modernity. The first phase is characterized by industrialization and the drive to conquer the natural world, the belief in progress and the disenchantment with religion, legitimized by opposing grand narratives of social and political change. Risk society marks the end of the first phase. Modernity is now 'freeing itself from the contours of classical industrial society' and emerging in a new form. The second phase of modernity is taking shape, but we cannot understand or describe it with our existing vocabulary. We do, however, become slowly conscious that although things still look the same and have the same form, behind the scenes they are not working in the way we have come to expect.

How we deal with this becomes a political problem with at least two solutions. If we see it as the consequence of a breakdown of traditional order, we may seek to preserve and strengthen those institutions and relationships that once worked, in the interests of social cohesion, to provide a secure backdrop to social, economic and political life. This politics appears to be a resistance to change. It builds on an idealized notion of community and encourages efforts to bring back the traditional family, reconstruct strong neighbourhoods and reassert a kind of commonsense morality to hold it all together. It offers a way of imagining a secure society. But this security is based on how people *should* live and on the obligations they *should* feel towards each other. It endeavours to build the ideas of trust and responsibility into institutions that are themselves rapidly changing and are incapable of responding as we imagine they used to. In trying to rebuild a world that we can take for granted, we succeed only in constructing a rhetoric or facade of certainty and common sense over the intense activity of change.

In contrast, the politics of risk society takes the reality of everyday life as its starting point, recognizing that we need a new language to describe what is happening to us. This language is not yet formulated, but it has to be a language that resonates with our experience and can take us forward into the unknown, opening up the possibility of living creatively with risk and uncertainty. It offers an alternative strategy to the politics of nostalgic community. The language of the family becomes less about form and more about the kinds of relationships that give children the love and security they need to become autonomous adults. The language of politics moves beyond assertions of competence, becoming less rigid in its definitions and more accessible to everybody. If the focus is shifted towards understanding the process of change and working with it rather than resisting it, the new parameters of politics can begin to emerge.

To do this we must look beyond the facade. Ulrich Beck and Anthony Giddens map the contours of this new society and the other contributors to this volume offer insights into the risks and possibilities that emerge when we step outside traditional approaches to uncertainty and begin to see things in a different way.

Adam Raphael's chapter on Lloyd's and the 'limits of insurance' reveals what can happen to institutions when they struggle to stand still while the world around them is changing. He charts the breakdown of the trust which had been the guiding principle of Lloyd's for over a century, following the massive losses made by its underwriters. Giddens has pointed to the misunderstanding that arises when we use old concepts to describe new situations. As he says, the troubles at Lloyd's 'were popularly portrayed as being bound up with class . . . In fact, they had their basic origin in the changing character of risk.' There was a failure to take account of the influence of global climatic change on 'natural disasters', and of the research that had been throwing doubt on the safety of asbestos since the beginning of the century. Lloyd's had continued to insure American corporations against asbestos risk up to the 1960s. Behind the patina of tradition and facade of certainty, the new dynamics of risk were taking effect.

Risk society, Giddens tells us, exists 'after nature and after tradition'. Living 'after nature', our previous attempts to control and transform natural processes in the interest of progress begin to reflect back on us. In his chapter *Nature Bites Back*, John Gray explores the relationship between technology and nature in the light of Chernobyl and the BSE crisis. We become aware of the implications of scientific and technological decisions taken in an effort to harness nuclear energy and to find cheaper ways to feed our cattle. We might not have foreseen the consequences of those decisions, but we were in effect producing the risks now characterizing the kind of society in which we live. In the same way, tuberculosis, once thought to have been controlled, is on the increase. Superbugs are becoming immune to antibiotics. In risk society we are confronted with the consequences of our actions – with the consequences, Gray points out, of our pride and inability to recognize and respect the fragility of the world we seek to control. There is a mismatch, Martin Woollacott suggests, between the way that such risks are coming to define the nature of modern life and the means of assessing and negotiating risks which still rely on the old, closed alliance between science, industry and government.

Robin Grove-White points to the political crisis this generates. While government and politicians fail to recognize the significance of these new risks, a growing public scepticism begins to challenge political legitimacy. What we need, he suggests, is a shared recognition of new forms of risk and uncertainty and a political commitment to widening the political process to include public participation in decisions about risk. In the case of biotechnology, for example, the risks of genetic intervention are not yet fully understood, yet science and industry, encouraged by government, continue to develop genetic technology while the public are, by and large, kept in ignorance. Meanwhile, ministers hide behind the traditional authority of scientific knowledge, waiting for conclusive proof of risk before taking preventative action.

As a way of overcoming this stalemate, the *precautionary principle* is explored by Stephen Tindale. It is a political mechanism which enables politicians to take precautionary action in situations where there is any reasonable doubt of risk to public health or the environment, without waiting for conclusive scientific proof. Since we cannot predict what the effects of genetic engineering will be, for example, the precautionary principle suggests that we should not proceed. Yet, as Tindale points out, we procrastinate and, like Dr Pangloss, expect that all will be well in the end. The greatest example of procrastination, Tindale suggests, is in respect of global warming. While there is a remarkable degree of consensus among experts as to the existence of global warming and its effects on climate change, governments still plead 'uncertainty' as an excuse to postpone decisions.

Living 'after tradition', Giddens tells us, 'is essentially to be in a world where life is no longer lived as fate'. We come to recognize through experience that we can no longer rely on experts to guide us in the choices we make and are forced to make decisions in the light of conflicting information. Science is losing its traditional role as expert adviser. We have become sceptical and have moved beyond the time when scientists in white coats could be trusted. Yet, as John Durant points outs, 'listening to current Government pronouncements about BSE is like living in a time warp; it is as if thirty years of questioning and criticism had simply not taken place.' This is why we do not trust politicians and experts: because they are ignoring the dynamic, keeping up the facade, because they do not know how to say that they don't know. Durant makes a plea for the policy-making process to respond to public awareness of risk, by acknowledging ignorance and uncertainty and drawing experts, policy-makers and the public into a mature debate of the issues.

As scientific information becomes increasingly ambiguous, there is a strong impulse to turn to what we see as more certain forms of knowledge and understanding, as external reference points which offer more security. Religion, morality and the politics of authority offer one way back to a world we can trust and in which we feel safe. But there has also been a renewed fascination, as Pat Kane points out, in myth, magic and extraterrestrial life. While some have argued that with this trend we are in danger of slipping into a 'New Dark Ages, in which scientific reason is derided and magic thinking reigns', Kane suggests that science will have to come to terms with 'ambiguity and mystery', to take on the possibility of unreason as part of its character, heralding the emergence of a new scientific paradigm.

Patricia Hewitt takes an optimistic look at the impact of the convergence of information and communications technology and its role in generating a new society and a new politics. She argues that the powerful networks involved are, like the printing press, inherently democratic. They have the power to destabilize existing social, economic and political structures and to create new ones. Networks generate new forms of political participation through a more open-ended and fluid form of dialogue: new communities across different dimensions of time and space, and new patterns of work which can be empowering, even though they may also generate real insecurities. We should not assume, Hewitt suggests, that the newly emerging, technologically generated social structures will conform to familiar hierarchies between the 'information haves' and the 'information have-nots'. Our assumptions about relationships, capabilities and opportunities are challenged by this technology, which seems to carry infinite enabling possibilities, but also has the capacity to be disabling. In this way, it is not the technology itself that will determine the character of our society, but our decisions about how we use it – which is, of course, up to politics.

Susie Orbach uncovers the internal dynamic which characterizes the politics of risk society, showing that it is the content of relationships between individuals that determines their capacity to thrive and enjoy life, rather than the formal structures that now appear to be breaking down. She says that we should not make assumptions as to the cause of despair felt by individuals in emotional distress, but look at it with fresh eyes. It is easy to understand the appeal of political nostalgia for the security of the family of the immediate postwar period; we can all relate to the search for certainty, for stability, for security. Rather than prescribe a model of family life to which people must try to conform, successfully or not, politicians might turn their attention to the content and quality of the attachments family members develop with each other as the focus for policy-making. Again, politics needs to connect with the way people really live their lives, and enhance it, rather than dictate how they *should* live. In acknowledging that emotional security is the basis of autonomy, we recognize the importance of building enabling relationships with those close to us. If people are involved in shaping the society they live in, they engage with everyday life and the risks they face, rather than feel themselves to be 'constantly reactive, blown off course' and rushing to catch up.

As politicians search for the key to social cohesion, Ray Pahl's chapter on friendship offers a new perspective on the kinds of relationship that might provide the 'social glue' they seem to be searching for. He challenges the taken-for-granted idea that families should be the providers of stability and security in society, and suggests that friendship networks can offer a more stable and enabling set of relationships. As a sociologist, Pahl seeks to focus on the *actual* pattern of social relationships in which people are involved. In a society increasingly characterized by risk and uncertainty in everyday life, people are beginning to search outside the traditional sources of security, increasing their reliance on friends. Friendship attachments differ according to expectation. We may not tell our intimate secrets to the friend with whom we play tennis, but there is a particular type of friendship which helps to build secure identities and can see us through many of the hurdles that life has in store. This friendship, Pahl suggests, is 'about knowing and being known. It is about communication. It is liberating and it is fundamentally egalitarian.' This 'pure friendship', he says, is 'a reflection of the contemporary concern for individuality', in that the commitments individuals make to each other are freely chosen and do not rest on family obligation. A society based on this type of relationship, which Pahl sees as becoming more common, will be a *friendly society*, cohesive, since the friendships arise out of real choice, and enabling, since they are based on reciprocal commitment.

Anna Coote points to the political charade in which we engage, putting us in a child-to-adult relationship with our politicians. We expect politicians to answer our questions and protect us from the hazards of life; rather like troublesome teenagers, we'll expect them to be infallible, yet we know they are not and consequently despise them. The politics of risk society, however, requires a relationship between the public, experts and politicians in which mutual respect and democratic dialogue replace the blind faith and mutual contempt which have characterized the political process. Authentic, or 'active' trust, as Giddens has described it, comes from democratic engagement and open dialogue through which all concerned have a stake in the decision-making process. In risk society, Anna Coote writes, public policy must engage in 'long-term planning for uncertainty' in which informed and active citizens enjoy a mature, adult-to-adult relationship with politicians and experts. Such a 'high-trust democracy' moves beyond a retreat into nostalgic authoritarianism or putting all our faith in the market.

Beneath the authoritarian response, Coote detects a desire to replace politics, which is about negotiating change, with a semblance of morality which is about conserving absolute values. Values, she argues, must resonate with the real, changing world we live in and be understood and shared as widely as possible. Of course it is tempting to go back, but the challenge is to resist the comfort of reconstructing old certainties and to build a new politics that goes beyond a reliance on moral absolutes – that itself takes a 'risk' and a leap into the unknown.

Risk society is forcing us to make decisions. The politics which asserts old certainties says that other people will make those decisions for us. The politics of risk society is more demanding. It demands active participation through all layers of social, political and economic activity. In risk society, as Martin Woollacott reminds us, 'risks are not just moments of danger as we forge forward: they are the process itself.' To engage with this process, we need a new public policy – its parameters are discussed in this book. They include, as Woollacott suggests, direct and continuous dialogue between the public, experts and politicians about 'the decisions which lead to risks being taken'. They include, Tindale writes, an effective use of the precautionary principle, so that we can all engage creatively with risk. They include, as Orbach and Pahl show, a positive understanding of the changing nature of personal and institutional relationships and a direct connection between policy initiatives and the reality of people's lives. In risk society, we need policy initiatives which give space to a new politics, still emerging, generated by uncertainty, which insists that decisions which affect us are taken in the context of democratic debate.

To move from day to day, from year to year, from century to century, we need to project into the future, to have some sense of what will happen to us and the world around us. Yet we seem to be deprived of the certainty we need to negotiate the future in a creative way. The politics of risk society releases us from this anxiety because we are acting *with* uncertainty and not denying it. It encourages action built on realistic assumptions, pushes out the boundaries of consensus and opens up the dynamic of action and debate. Politics *is* changing. It remains for politicians to open their eyes to the possibilities of risk society.

1

Politics of Risk Society

ULRICH BECK

Consider the intellectual situation in Europe after 1989. A whole world order had broken down. What an opportunity to adventure into the new! But we stick to old concepts and ideas, and make the same mistakes. There is even a kind of left protectionism and a switch of position. As Anthony Giddens has pointed out, radical socialism has become conservative and conservatism has become radical.[1] We have to rediscover this crazy, mad-cow disease world sociologically, and the script of modernity has to be rewritten, redefined, reinvented. This is what the theory of world risk society is about, and to give you a better idea of my 'mistakes', I will concentrate on three points.[2]

First, I shall return to the theory of risk society, to show how it conveys a new conception of a 'non-industrial' society and how it modifies social theory and politics. Secondly, I shall take the position of my critics and explore what I see as the theoretical issues which now limit the development of my ideas on risk. Thirdly, I shall point to the theoretical and political avenues that I should like to see explored, perhaps on a comparative and European level.

Britain is experiencing what *The Independent* has called 'beef-gate' – the shock of living in a risk society. Society has become a laboratory where there is absolutely nobody in charge. An experiment has been inflicted on us by the beef industries, and the most ordinary decision – to eat or not to eat beef – could be a life and death decision. Hamlet has to be reconsidered: to beef or not to beef, now is the question! Sociologically, there is a big difference between those who take risks and those who are victimized by risks others take. I shall point to a few epistemological principles which characterize the three main arguments of the theory of risk society.

Risk society begins where nature ends.[3] As Giddens has pointed out, this is where we switch the focus of our anxieties from what nature can do to us to what we have done to nature. The BSE crisis is not simply a matter of fate but a matter of decisions and options, science and politics, industries, markets and capital. This is not an outside risk but a risk generated right inside each person's life and inside a variety of institutions. A central paradox of risk society is that these internal risks are generated by the processes of modernization which try to control them.

Risk society begins where tradition ends, when, in all spheres of life, we can no longer take traditional certainties for granted. The less we can rely on traditional securities, the more risks we have to negotiate. The more risks, the more decisions and choices we have to make. There is an important line of argument which connects the theory of risk society, in this context, to complementary processes of individualization in the spheres of work, family life and self-identity, which I have explored elsewhere.[4]

The theory of risk society interprets the ways in which these two states of interconnected processes, the end of nature and the end of tradition, have altered the epistemological and cultural status of science and the constitution of politics. In the age of risk, society becomes a laboratory with nobody responsible for the outcomes of experiments. The private sphere's creation of risks means that it can no longer be considered apolitical. Indeed, a whole arena of hybrid subpolitics emerges in the realms of investment decisions, product development, plant management and scientific research priorities. In this situation, the conventional political forces and representations of industrial society have been sidelined.[5] Let's look at these principles in more detail.

The notion of risk society clarifies a world characterized by the loss of a clear distinction between nature and culture. Today, if we talk about nature we talk about culture and if we talk about culture we talk about nature. When we think of global warming, the hole in the ozone layer, pollution or food scares, nature is inescapably contaminated by human activity. This common danger has a levelling effect that whittles away some of the carefully erected boundaries between classes, nations, humans and the rest of nature, between creators of culture and creatures of instinct, or to use an earlier distinction, between beings with and those without a soul.

We live in a *hybrid* world which transcends old theoretical distinctions, as Bruno Latour has convincingly argued.[6] Risks are *man-made hybrids*. They include and combine politics, ethics, mathematics, mass media, technologies, cultural definitions and precepts. In risk society, modern society becomes reflexive, that is, becomes both an issue and a problem for itself.

Many sociologists (including Foucault, or Adorno and Horkheimer, critical theorists of the Frankfurt School) pictured modernity as a prison house of technical knowledge. We are all, to alter the metaphor, small cogs in the gigantic machine of technical and bureaucratic reasons. Yet risk society, in opposition to the image of the term, captures a world which is much more open and contingent than any classical concept of modern society suggests – and is so precisely *because of* and not *in spite of* the knowledge that we have accumulated about ourselves and about the material environment.

As François Ewald argues,[7] risk is a way of controlling or, one could say, colonizing the future. Events that do *not* exist (yet) strongly influence our present affairs and actions. So risks are a kind of virtual, yet real, reality. The greater the threat (or to be more precise, the social definition and construction of the threat), the greater the obligation and power to change current events. Let us take 'globalization risk' as an example. It says, if you want to survive in the global capitalistic market, you have to change the basic foundations of modernity: social security, the nation-state, the power of the unions and so on. The greater the threat, the greater the change which has to be undertaken in order to control the future. This deeply politicizing meaning of the risk society argument can be used not only by environmentalists but also by global capital, and more effectively too. As Giddens and I have pointed out, there is another central paradox that we have to understand, which is that the more we try to colonize the future, the more likely it is to spring surprises on us. This is why the notion of risk moves through two stages.

In the first instance, risk seems no more than a part of an essential calculus, a means of sealing off boundaries as the future is invaded. Risk makes the unforeseeable foreseeable, or promises to do so. In this initial form, risk is a statistical part of the operation of insurance companies.[8] They know a lot about the secrets of risk which change society, even though nothing has yet happened. This is risk in a world where much remains as 'given', as fate, including external nature and those forms of social life coordinated by tradition. As nature becomes permeated by industrialization and as tradition is dissolved, new types of incalculability emerge. We move then into the second stage of risk, which Giddens[9] and I have called *manufactured uncertainty*. Here the production of risks is the consequence of scientific and political efforts to control or minimize them.

There are two aspects to this. There was once a time when a risk was something you indulged in for a bit of excitement. A bet on the Grand National, a spin of the wheel – it was all meant to add a bit of spice to an otherwise orderly and predictable life. Now manufactured uncertainty means that risk has become an inescapable part of our lives and everybody is facing unknown and barely calculable risks. Risk becomes another word for 'nobody knows.'[10] We no longer choose to take risks, we have them thrust upon us. We are living on a ledge – in a random risk society, from which nobody can escape. Our society has become riddled with random risks. Calculating and managing risks which nobody really knows has become one of our main preoccupations. That used to be a specialist job for actuaries, insurers and scientists. Now we all have to engage in it, with whatever rusty tools we can lay our hands on – sometimes the calculator, sometimes the astrology column. The basic question here is: how can we make decisions about a risk we know nothing about? Should we ignore it and possibly get hurt or killed? Or should we be alarmed and stop or exclude all likely causes? Which course of action is 'rational', the first or the second option?

On the other hand, manufactured uncertainty means that the source of the most troubling new risks we face is something most of us would regard as unequivocally beneficial – our expanding knowledge. It is partly because we know more about the brain that we now know that people in a persistent vegetative state may be conscious and so should not have their life support machines turned off. Yet, as scientific knowledge opens up new opportunities for us, it also makes the world more complex and unknowable, at least by any one individual, often for experts too. How many hamburgers do you need to eat to catch the deadly CJD? Fifty, a hundred, two hundred, a thousand? In what amount of time? Two of the first victims of CJD in Britain had been vegetarians for the five years before they caught it – before that, they had been addicted to hamburgers.

As knowledge and technology race ahead, we are left behind panting in ignorance, increasingly unable to understand or control the machines we depend on and so less able to calculate the consequences of their going wrong. Environmental science has encouraged us to be less short-term in our thinking. We now worry about the consequence of our actions for future generations in far-flung places. But this admirable long-termism also makes it more difficult to calculate the risks of our decisions. What is the risk that your grandchildren's environment will suffer if you use that aerosol or car too much?

Many believe that in the age of risk there can be only one authority left, and that is science. But this is not only a complete misunderstanding of science, it is also a complete misunderstanding of the notion of risk. It is not failure but success which has demonopolized science. One could even say that the more successful sciences have been in this century, the more they have reflected upon their own limits of certainty, the more they have been transformed into a source of manufactured reflexive uncertainty. Sciences are operating in terms of probabilities, which do not exclude the worst case.

This is even more true in identifying and managing risk. In the case of risk conflicts, politicians can no longer rely on scientific experts. This is so, first, because there are always competing and conflicting claims and viewpoints from a variety of actors and affected groups who define risks very differently.[11] So producing conflicting knowledge on risk is a matter of good and not bad experts. Secondly, experts can only supply more or less uncertain factual information about probabilities, but never answer the question: which risk is acceptable and which is not. Thirdly, if politicians just implement scientific advice, they become *caught in the mistakes, modes and uncertainties of scientific knowledge*. So the lesson of the risk society is this: politics and morality are gaining – have to gain! – priority over shifting scientific reasoning.

There used to be a clear division between research and theory, on the one hand, and technology, on the other. The logic of scientific discovery presupposes testing before putting into practice. This is breaking down in the age of risky technologies.[12] Nuclear technologies have to be built *in order* to study their functioning and risks. Test-tube babies have to be born *in order* to find out about the theories and assumptions of biotechnologies. Genetically engineered plants have to be grown *in order* to test the theory. The controllability of the laboratory situation is lost. This causes serious problems.

Scientists are becoming lay persons. They do not know what will happen before they begin their research. At the same time they need the support of the politicians and the public to finance their research and for this reason they have to claim that everything is under control and nothing can go wrong.

As Karl Popper once said, the basic rationality of science is that we should learn from our mistakes. In risk society, mistakes mean that nuclear reactors leak or explode, test-tube babies are born deformed, people are killed by CJD. So scientists cannot make mistakes any more, sorry. But they *do* make mistakes and more than ever they reflect upon them.

Society becomes a laboratory, but there is no one responsible for its outcomes. Experiments in nuclear energy and biotechnology, for example, become inconclusive in the dimensions of time, space and the number of people involved. There is, however, no experimenter in charge, no decision-maker to decide on the validity of the initial hypothesis with scientific authority.

So what is the role of politics? The fact is that no direct decisions are made about technology in the political system (with an exception of nuclear power plants). But on the other hand, if anything goes wrong, the political institutions are made responsible for decisions they didn't take and for consequences and threats they know nothing about.

In relation to the state and Parliament, industry possesses a double advantage. It has autonomy in investment decisions and a monopoly on the application of technology. Politicians are in a bad position, struggling to catch up with what is going on in technological development. Most MPs get their information about technological developments through the media; in spite of all the support for research, the political influence on the goals of technological development remains secondary. No votes are taken in Parliament on the employment and development of micro-electronics, genetic technology and the like. Most of the time, MPs vote in support of them in order to protect the country's economic future and jobs. Thus the division of power leaves the industries with the role of primary decision-maker without responsibility for risks to the public. Meanwhile, politics is assigned the task of democratically legitimizing decisions that it has not taken and doesn't know about, especially since the privatization of industries which were previously run by the state. What happens to the security standards of the privatized railway system? Of privately run nuclear power plants? Has the state really shed the responsibility in the eyes of the public?

So, risks are nobody's responsibility. Neurotechnologies and genetic engineering are reshaping the laws that govern the human mind and life. Who is doing this? Scientific experts? Politicians? Industries? The public? Ask any of them and the reply will be in each case: nobody. Risk politics resembles the 'nobody's rule' that Hannah Arendt tells us is the most tyrannical of all forms of power, because under such circumstances nobody can be held responsible. In the case of risk conflicts, bureaucracies are suddenly unmasked and the alarmed public becomes aware of what they really are: *forms of organized irresponsibility.*[13]

Given that risks are no longer attributable to external agency, industrial societies have developed institutions and rules for coping with unforeseen, unintended consequences and the risks they produce. The welfare state can be seen as a collective and institutional response to the nature of localized risks and dangers, based on principles of rule-governed attribution of fault and blame, legally implemented compensation, actuarial insurance principles and collectively shared responsibility. The classic example of this would be the creation of compensation and insurance schemes for accident and injury at work and unemployment.

However, under the impact of modern risks and manufactured uncertainties, these modes of determining and perceiving risk, attributing causality and allocating compensation have irreversibly broken down, throwing the function and legitimacy of modern bureaucracies, states, economies and science into question. Risks that were calculable under industrial society become incalculable and unpredictable in the risk society. Compared to the possibilities of adjudging blame and causality in classical modernity, the world risk society possesses no such certainties or guarantees.

In terms of social politics, the ecological crisis involves a systematic violation, or crisis, of basic rights, and the long-term impact of this weakening of society can scarcely be overestimated. For dangers are being produced by industry, externalized by economics, individualized by the legal system, legitimized by the sciences and made to appear harmless by politics. That this is breaking down the power and credibility of institutions only becomes clear when the system is put on the spot, as Greenpeace, for example, has tried to do. The result is the subpoliticization of world society.

In the second part of my paper, I shall switch sides to tell you about some of the refutations my risk society theory has provoked. In a conference in Cardiff in March 1996 Professor Hilary Rose said that she felt that risk society had a distinctly German background and that Britain could not afford to be a risk society. To her, the theory of risk society presumes a degree of wealth and security typical of postwar Germany. It is certainly one of the very few attempts to open up the social sciences and social theory to ecological questions, and it is the case that being 'green' is part of the German national identity. On the other hand, testing atomic weapons may be part of the French national identity, and eating roast beef on a Sunday lunchtime may be part of the British culture. Who knows? The important point to make here is that risk conflicts are not only intracultural conflicts. They cross cultural boundaries and are even more conflicts of contradictory certainties. People, expert groups, cultures, nations are having to get involved with each other whether they like it or not. It may not be completely wrong to say that a European public has been born, unintentionally and involuntarily, over the conflict over British beef. It is the 'mad-cow disease Europe' where everybody is quarrelling with everybody else, not only on a general technocratic level but also on an everyday level. If you visit, for example, a *Wirthaus* (a small local restaurant) in southern Bavaria and read the menu you will find a photograph of the local farmer and his family trying to build up trust in his 'good' beef which has nothing to do with the 'bad' British beef.

So, as Barbara Adams argues,[14] a distinction between knowledge and impact can be made which leads to a distinction between two phases of risk society. In the first phase, which we can call 'residual risk society', the impacts are systematically produced, are not the subject of public knowledge and debate and are not at the centre of political conflict. This phase is dominated by the self-identity of 'goods' of industrial and technological progress, which simultaneously intensifies and legitimizes as 'residual risks' hazards resulting from decisions. In the second phase, a completely different situation arises, when the hazards of industrial society dominate public and private debates. Now the institutions of industrial society produce and legitimize hazards which they cannot control. During this transition, property and power relationships remain constant and industrial society sees and criticizes itself *as* risk society. In the first phase, society still makes decisions and acts on the pattern of simple modernity. In the second phase, debates and conflicts which originate in the dynamic of risk society are being superimposed on interest organizations, the legal system and politics. So modernity becomes reflexive.

In all my books I try to demonstrate that the return to the theoretical and political philosophy of simple modernity, in the age of global risk, is doomed to failure. Those orthodox theories and politics remain tied to notions of progress and benign technological change, tied to the belief that the risks we face can still be captured by nineteenth-century, scientific models of hazard assessment and industrial notions of hazard and safety. Simultaneously, the disintegrating institutions of industrial modernity – nuclear families, stable labour markets, segregated gender roles, social classes – can be shored up and buttressed against the waves of reflexive modernization sweeping the West. This dominant attempt to apply nineteenth-century ideas to the late twentieth century is the *category mistake* of social theory, social sciences and politics. It is this point which I try to make in all my work. So let me sharpen this central idea and mention the core notions of *organized irresponsibility*, the *relations of definition*, and the *social explosiveness of hazards*.

The idea of *organized irresponsibility* helps to explain how and why the institutions of modern society must unavoidably acknowledge the reality of catastrophe while simultaneously denying its existence, cover its origins and preclude compensation or control. To put it another way, risk societies are characterized by the paradox of more and more environmental degradation, perceived and possible, and an expansion of environmental law and regulation. Yet at the same time no individual or institution seems to be held specifically accountable for anything. How can this be? To me the key to explaining this state of affairs is the mismatch that exists in risk society between the character of hazards, or manufactured uncertainties, produced by late industrial society and the prevalent *relations of definition*[15] which date in their construction and content from an early and qualitatively different epoch.

The notion of relations of definition is the parallel notion to the relations of production (Karl Marx) in the risk society. They include the rules, institutions and capacities that structure the identification and assessment of risks; they are the legal, epistemological and cultural matrix in which risk politics is conducted. I focus here on four relations of definition:

1 Who is to determine the harmfulness of products or the danger of risks? Is the responsibility with those who generate those risks, with those who benefit from them, or with public agencies?
2 What kind of knowledge or non-knowledge about the causes, dimensions, actors, etc., is involved? To whom does that 'proof' have to be submitted?
3 What is to count as sufficient proof in a world in which we necessarily deal with contested knowledge and probabilities?
4 If there are dangers and damages, who is to decide on compensation for the afflicted and on appropriate forms of future control and regulation?[16]

In relation to each of these questions, risk societies are currently trapped in a vocabulary that lends itself to an interrogation of the risks and hazards through the relations of definition of simple, classic, first modernity. These are singularly inappropriate not only for modern catastrophes, but also for the challenges of manufactured uncertainties. Consequently we have to face the paradox that at the very time when threats and hazards are seen to become more dangerous and more obvious, they simultaneously slip through the net of proofs, attributions and compensation with which the legal and political systems attempt to capture them.

Of course, everybody asks who is the *political subject* of risk society? I have put a lot of thought into answering this question, but my answer has not yet been acknowledged theoretically or politically.[17] My argument is as follows: nobody is the subject and everybody is the subject at the same time. It might not be very surprising to you that this answer has not been recognized. But there is more to it. What I propose comes very close to Bruno Latour's theory of quasi-objects.[18] To me the hazards themselves are quasi-subjects; this acting-active quality is produced by the *contradictions in which institutions get caught up in risk societies*. I use a metaphor to explain this idea: the *social explosiveness of hazard*. It explores the ways in which awareness of large-scale hazards, risks and manufactured uncertainties sets off a dynamic of cultural and political change that undermines state bureaucracies, challenges the dominance of science and redraws the boundaries and battle-lines of contemporary politics. So hazards, understood as *socially constructed and produced 'quasi–subjects'*, are a powerful uncontrollable 'actor' to delegitimize and destabilize state institutions with responsibilities for pollution control, in particular, and public safety in general.

Hazards themselves sweep away the attempts of institutional elites and experts to control them. Governments and bureaucracies, of course, exercise well-worn routines of denial. Data can be hidden, denied and distorted. The gap between knowledge and impact can be exploited. Counter-arguments can be mobilized. Expert-systems can be adjusted. Maximum permissible levels of acceptance can be raised. Human error, rather than systematic risk, can be cast as the villain of the piece and so on. And last but not least, Europe can be made responsible for the mad-cow disease crisis. However, states are fighting a battle where victories are temporary because they offer nineteenth-century pledges of security to the age of world risk society. We can see this happening all around us.

These ideas are, of course, bound to the notion of the *safety* or *provident* state, to be found in the work of François Ewald.[19] To me, his theory represents a basic shift in the interpretation of the welfare state. While the majority of social scientists have sought to explain the origins and construction of the welfare state in terms of class interests, the maintenance of social order or the enhancement of national productivity and military power, this argument understands the provision of services (health care), the creation of insurance schemes (pensions and unemployment insurance) and the regulation of the economy and the environment in terms of the creation of security. In relation to industries and technologies, of course, technical experts do play a central role in answering the question of how safe is safe enough. This model of the modern capitalist state as a provident state has been challenged. One of the critiques is that the notion of a safety state is much more closely correlated with the institutions and procedures of continental Western European states than with either the states of Anglo-American capitalism or the social democratic states of Scandinavia.

Finally, I should like to point to two implications of this thesis. The first is that risk society is not about exploding nuclear submarines falling out of the sky; it is not, as you might assume, one more expression of the 'German angst' at the millennium. Quite the opposite. What I suggest is a new model for understanding our times, in a not unhopeful spirit. What others see as the development of a postmodern order, my argument interprets as a stage of radicalized modernity. A stage where the dynamics of individualization, globalization and risk undermine modernity and its foundations. Whatever happens, modernity gets *reflexive*, that means concerned with its unintended consequences, risks and foundations.[20] Where most postmodern theorists are critical of grand narratives, general theory and humanity, I remain committed to all of these, but in a new sense. To me, Enlightenment is not a historical notion and set of ideas, but a process and dynamic where criticism, self-criticism, irony and humanity play a central role (the theme of my current research). Where for many philosophers and sociologists 'rationality' means 'discourse' and 'cultural relativism', my notion of 'reflexive modernity' implies that we do not have *enough* reason (*Vernunft*).

Secondly, previously depoliticized areas of decision-making are getting politicized through the perception of risk, and must be opened to public scrutiny and debate. Corporate economic decisions, scientific research agendas, plans for the development and deployment of new technologies must all be opened up to a generalized process of discussion, and a legal and institutional framework for their democratic legitimation must be developed.[21]

To me, technical (or ecological) democracy is the utopia of a responsible modernity, a vision of society in which the consequences of technological development and economic change are debated before the key decisions are taken. The burden of proof regarding future risks and hazards and current environment degradation would lie with the perpetrators rather than the injured party: from the polluter *pays* principle to the polluter *proves* principle. Finally, a new body of standards of proof, correctness, truth and agreement in science and law must be established. So what we need is nothing less than a *second Enlightenment* which opens up our minds, eyes and institutions to the self-afflicted endangerment of industrial civilization.

Many theories and theorists do not recognize the *opportunities* of risk society. Moreover, we have to recognize the ways in which contemporary debates of this sort – by which the nuclear and biotechnology industries, for example, have been forced to justify and defend their activities in the public domain[22] – are constrained by the epistemological and legal systems within which they are conducted.

So this could be one of the themes which I would like to see explored, maybe on a comparative and European level. It implies that we reconstruct the social definition of risks and risk management in different cultural frameworks; that we find out about the (negative) power of risk conflicts and definitions in contexts where people are forced together who do not want to speak to each other, but still have to. All this is familiar and already takes place. But to combine it with the questions of organized irresponsibility and the relations of definition in different European cultures and states might be worthwhile and a new adventure.

Notes

1 A. Giddens, *Beyond Left and Right* (Polity Press, Cambridge, 1994).
2 In this chapter, I shall attempt to summarize my argument on risk society; I have found it most stimulating to read the comments in David Goldblatt's chapter, 'The Sociology of Risk: Ulrich Beck', in D. Goldblatt, *Social Theory and the Environment* (Polity Press, Cambridge, 1996), pp. 184–203.
3 U. Beck, *Risk Society* (Sage, London, 1992), pp. 80–4.
4 Ibid., part 2, and U. Beck and E. Beck-Gernsheim, 'Individualization and Precarious Freedoms: Perspectives and Controversies of a Subject-Orientated Sociology', in P. Heelas, S. Lash and P. Morris (eds), *Detraditionalization* (Blackwell, Oxford, 1996), pp. 23–48.
5 U. Beck, *The Reinvention of Politics* (Polity Press, Cambridge, 1997).
6 B. Latour, *Wir sind niemals modern gewesen* (Academie Verlag, Berlin, 1995).
7 F. Ewald, *L'État Providence* (Grasser & Fasquelle, Paris, 1987).
8 Ibid.
9 Giddens, *Beyond Left and Right*.
10 U. Beck, 'Misunderstanding Reflexivity', in Beck, *Democracy without Enemies* (Polity Press, Cambridge, 1998).
11 B. Wynne, 'May the Sheep Safely Graze?', in S. Lash, B. Szerszynski and B. Wynne (eds), *Risk, Environment and Modernity* (Sage, London, 1996).
12 U. Beck, *Ecological Politics in an Age of Risk* (Polity Press, Cambridge, 1995), pp. 111–27.
13 Ibid., pp. 92–106, 133–46.
14 B. Adams, 'Timescapes of Modernity', manuscript, Cardiff, 1997.
15 Beck, *Ecological Politics*, pp. 116–18, 129–33, 136–7.
16 Goldblatt, *Social Theory*, pp. 166f.
17 Beck, *Ecological Politics*, pp. 96–110.
18 Latour, *Wir sind niemals modern gewesen*.
19 Ewald, *L'État Providence*.
20 U. Beck, A. Giddens and S. Lash, *Reflexive Modernization* (Polity Press, Cambridge, 1994).
21 Beck, *The Reinvention of Politics*.
22 E. Beck-Gernsheim, *The Social Implications of Bioengineering* (Humanities, Atlantic Highlands, NJ, 1995).

2

Risk Society: the Context of British Politics

ANTHONY GIDDENS

What do the following have in common: BSE; the troubles at Lloyd's; the Nick Leason affair; global warming; red wine as good for you; declining sperm counts? All reflect a vast swathe of change which we are experiencing in our lives today. Much of this change is bound up with the impact of science and technology on our everyday activities and on the material environment. The modern world, of course, has long been shaped by the influence of science and scientific discovery. As the pace of innovation hots up, however, new technologies penetrate more and more to the core of our lives; and more and more of what we feel and experience comes under the scientific spotlight.

The situation does not lead to increasing certainty about, or security, in the world – in some ways the opposite is true. As Karl Popper above all has shown, science does not produce proof and can never do more than approximate to truth. The founders of modern science believed it would produce knowledge built on firm foundations. Popper supposes, by contrast, that science is built on shifting sands. The first principle of scientific advance is that even one's most cherished theories and beliefs are always open to revision. Science is thus an inherently sceptical endeavour, involving a process of the constant revision of claims to knowledge.

The sceptical, mutable nature of science was for a long time insulated from the wider public domain – an insulation which persisted so long as science and technology were relatively restricted in their effects on everyday life. Today, we are all in regular and routine contact with these traits of scientific innovation. The consequences for health of drinking red wine, for example, were once seen by researchers as basically harmful. More recent research indicates that, taken in moderation, the health benefits of red wine outweigh the drawbacks. What will tomorrow's research show? Will it perhaps reveal that red wine is toxic after all?

We don't, and we can't, know – yet all of us, as consumers, have to respond in some way or another to this unstable and complex framework of scientific claims and counterclaims. Living in the UK, should one eat beef? Who can say? The health risk appears to be slight. Yet there is at least the possibility of an outbreak of BSE-related disease five, ten or twenty years from now among the human population.

We don't and can't know – the same applies to a diversity of new risk situations. Take, for instance, declining sperm counts. Some scientific studies make authoritative claims about increasing male infertility, and trace this to the action of environmental toxins. Other scientists, however, dispute the very existence of the phenomenon, let alone the explanations offered to account for it. Global warming is accepted as real by the majority of specialists in the area. Yet there is no shortage of experts who either deny that global warming exists or regard it as produced by long-term climatic fluctuations rather than by the greenhouse effect.

The Lloyd's insurance market seems for the moment to have got over the disastrous financial troubles which have plagued it over the last few years. Such troubles were popularly portrayed as being bound up with class – with the complacent outlook of the 'names' and their brokers. In fact, they had their basic origin in the changing character of risk. Lloyd's was hit by, among other things, findings about the toxic nature of asbestos and by a series of natural disasters – which were possibly not 'natural' at all, but influenced by global climatic change. The number of typhoons, hurricanes and other climatic disturbances happening in the world each year has climbed over the past fifteen years or so. With its massive futures commitments, Lloyd's – in common with other lesser insurance institutions – could be financially crippled at any time by as yet quite unforeseen negative consequences of new scientific findings or technological changes.

Simon Sebag Montefiore has written an interesting account of the adventures of Nick Leason and Barings Bank. Sebag Montefiore suggests that there are two different ways in which what happened at Barings can be interpreted (much like the events at Lloyd's). On the one hand, there is a class plus corruption explanation. According to this view, Barings Bank collapsed because it had a crusty, upper-class management at odds with the demands of a dynamic global economic order.

Sebag Montefiore casts doubt on this explanation. He argues that people working at the outer edges of the financial system, particularly in futures markets – complex markets where deals can be struck over movements in prices which have not yet, and may never, happen – are like astronauts. They have stepped outside the realm of bankers and financial experts – and they have stepped outside without a lifeline. Nick Leason drifted away much too far from any solid ground, but most others are able to keep themselves attached to their space capsule.

Sebag Montefiore has a very arresting phrase to describe this situation. He says Nick Leason and other people like him 'operate at the outer edge of the ordered world, on the barbaric final frontier of modern technology'. In other words, they are involved with systems which even they themselves do not understand, so dramatic is the onrush of change in the new electronic global economy. I think this is right, but the argument can be further generalized. It is not just people like Nick Leason, not just the new financial entrepreneurs, who live at the barbaric outer edge of modern technology. *All* of us now do – and I would take this to be the defining characteristic of what Ulrich Beck calls risk society. A risk society is a society where we increasingly live on a high technological frontier which absolutely no one completely understands and which generates a diversity of possible futures.

The origins of risk society can be traced to two fundamental transformations which are affecting our lives today. Each is connected to the increasing influence of science and technology, although not wholly determined by them. The first transformation can be called *the end of nature*; and the second *the end of tradition*.

The end of nature does not mean a world in which the natural environment disappears. It means that there are now few if any aspects of the physical world untouched by human intervention. The end of nature is relatively recent. It has come about over something like the last forty or fifty years, largely as a result of the intensification of technological change noted earlier.

It isn't something, of course, which can be precisely dated, but we can nevertheless roughly plot when the end of nature happened. It happened when a transition came about from the sort of anxieties people used to have about nature to a new set of worries. For hundreds of years, people worried about what nature could do to us – earthquakes, floods, plagues, bad harvests and so on. At a certain point, somewhere over the past fifty years or so, we stopped worrying so much about what nature could do to us, and we started worrying much more about what we have done to nature. That transition makes one major point of entry into risk society. It is a society which lives after nature.

However, it is also a society which lives after tradition. To live after the end of tradition is essentially to be in a world where life is no longer lived as fate. For many people – and this is still a source of class division in modern societies – diverse aspects of life were established by tradition as fate. It was the fate of a woman to be involved in a domestic milieu for much of her life, to have children and look after the house. It was the fate of men to go out to work, to work until they retired and then – quite often soon after retirement – essentially to fade away. We no longer live our lives as fate, in a process which Ulrich Beck calls individualization. A society which lives after nature and after tradition is really very different from the earlier form of industrial society – the basis for the development of the core intellectual traditions of Western culture.

To analyse what risk society is, one must make a series of distinctions. First of all, we must separate risk from hazard or danger. Risk is not, as such, the same as hazard or danger. A risk society is not intrinsically more dangerous or hazardous than pre-existing forms of social order. It is instructive in this context to trace out the origins of the term 'risk'. Life in the Middle Ages was hazardous; but there was no notion of risk and there doesn't seem in fact to be a notion of risk in any traditional culture. The reason for this is that dangers are experienced as given. Either they come from God, or they come simply from a world which one takes for granted. The idea of risk is bound up with the aspiration to control and particularly with the idea of controlling the future.

This observation is important. The idea of 'risk society' might suggest a world which has become more hazardous, but this is not necessarily so. Rather, it is a society increasingly preoccupied with the future (and also with safety), which generates the notion of risk. The idea of risk, interestingly, was first used by Western explorers when they ventured into new waters in their travels across the world. From exploring geographical space, it came to be transferred to the exploration of time. The word refers to a world which we are both exploring, and seeking to normalize and control. Essentially, 'risk' always has a negative connotation, since it refers to the chance of avoiding an unwanted outcome. But it can quite often be seen in a positive light, in terms of the taking of bold initiatives in the face of a problematic future. Successful risk-takers, whether in exploration, in business or in mountaineering, are widely admired.

We should distinguish risk from hazard, but we must also make a distinction between two kinds of risk. The first two hundred years of the existence of industrial society were dominated by what one might call *external risk*. External risk, expressed in down-to-earth terms, is risk of events that may strike individuals unexpectedly (from the outside, as it were), but that happen regularly enough and often enough in a whole population of people to be broadly predictable, and so insurable. There are two kinds of insurance associated with the rise of industrial society: the private insurance company and public insurance, which is the predominant concern of the welfare state.

The welfare state became the left's project in the post-1945 period – it became seen above all as a means of achieving social justice and income redistribution. By and large, however, it did not originate as such. It developed as a security state, a way of protecting against risk, where collective rather than private insurance was necessary. Like early forms of private insurance, it was built on the presumption of external risk. External risk can be fairly well calculated – one can draw up actuarial tables and decide on that basis how to insure people. Sickness, disablement, unemployment were treated by the welfare state as 'accidents of fate', against which insurance should be collectively provided.

A world which lives after nature and after the end of tradition is one marked by a transition from external to what I call *manufactured risk*. Manufactured risk is risk created by the very progression of human development, especially by the progression of science and technology. Manufactured risk refers to new risk environments for which history provides us with very little previous experience. We often don't really know what the risks are, let alone how to calculate them accurately in terms of probability tables.

Manufactured risk is expanding in most dimensions of human life. It is associated with a side of science and technology which the early theorists of industrial society by and large did not foresee. Science and technology create as many uncertainties as they dispel – and these uncertainties cannot be 'solved' in any simple way by yet further scientific advance. Manufactured uncertainty intrudes directly into personal and social life – it isn't confined to more collective settings of risk. In a world where one can no longer simply rely on tradition to establish what to do in a given range of contexts, people have to take a more active and risk-infused orientation to their relationships and involvements.

The rise of risk society has several interesting consequences – which should concern anyone who has taken an interest in the BSE debate in Britain and continental Europe, or in fact in any of the episodes I mentioned at the beginning of this discussion.

As manufactured risk expands – or, if you like, as we live more and more in a risk society in Ulrich Beck's terms – there is a new riskiness to risk. In a social order in which new technologies are chronically affecting our lives, and an almost endless revision of taken-for-granted ways of doing things ensues, the future becomes ever more absorbing, but at the same time opaque. There are few direct lines to it, only a plurality of 'future scenarios'.

We recently saw the tenth anniversary of the nuclear disaster at the Chernobyl plant. No one knows whether it is hundreds – or millions – of people who have been affected by the Chernobyl fall-out. The long-term effects will in any case be difficult to chart, because if they exist they are likely to be diffuse. We are altering the environment, and the patterns of life we follow, almost constantly. Even many apparently benign habits or innovations could turn sour – just as, conversely, risks can often be overestimated. Take the example of smoking. Smoking was encouraged by doctors up to some thirty or so years ago as a means of relaxation. No one knew the time bomb which the practice of smoking was stirring up. The BSE episode might have an opposite outcome. Perhaps it will turn out that humans are not affected. It is characteristic of the new types of risk that it is even disputed whether they exist at all.

In risk society there is a new moral climate of politics, one marked by a push-and-pull between accusations of scaremongering on the one hand and of cover-ups on the other. A good deal of political decision-making is now about managing risks – risks which do not originate in the political sphere, yet have to be politically managed. If anyone – government official, scientific expert or lay person – takes any given risk seriously, he or she must proclaim it. It must be widely publicized, because people must be persuaded that the risk is real – a fuss must be made about it. However, if a fuss is indeed created and the risk turns out to be minimal, those involved will be accused of scaremongering.

Suppose on the other hand that the authorities decide that the risk is not very great, as the British government did in the case of BSE. In this case, the government says: we've got the backing of scientists here; there isn't much risk, we can go on as we did before. Yet if things turn out otherwise, then of course they will be accused of a cover-up.

Paradoxically, scaremongering may be necessary to reduce risks we face – yet if it is 'successful' in this sense, it appears as just that, scaremongering. The case of AIDS is an example. Suppose governments and experts make great public play with the risks associated with unsafe sex, to get people to change their sexual behaviour. Suppose then that many people do change their sexual behaviour and AIDS does not spread nearly as much as originally predicted. The response is likely to be: why were you scaring everyone like that? This sort of political dilemma becomes routine in risk society, but there is no easily available way of confronting it. For as I mentioned earlier, even whether there are any risks at all is likely to be controversial. We just cannot know beforehand when we are actually 'scaremongering' and when we are not.

Third, the emergence of risk society is not wholly about the avoidance of hazards, for reasons also given previously. Risk has positive aspects to it. Risk society, looked at positively, is one in which there is an expansion of choice. Now obviously choice is differentially distributed according to class and income. As nature and tradition release their hold, for instance, some otherwise infertile women can pay to have children through the use of new reproductive technologies, whereas others cannot. We know that in detraditionalized social settings some women live in poverty after divorce, whereas others achieve a more rewarding life than they could have done before. Technological innovation usually expands the domain of choice; as does the disappearance of tradition. As customary ways of doing things become problematic, people must choose in many areas which used to be governed by taken-for-granted norms. Eating is an example: there are no traditional diets any more.

The advent of risk society has strong implications for rethinking the political agenda in this country and elsewhere. The emergence of manufactured risk presumes a new politics because it presumes a reorientation of values and the strategies relevant to pursuing them. There is no risk which can even be described without reference to a value. That value may be simply the preservation of human life, although it is usually more complex. When there is a clash of the different types of risk, there is a clash of values and a directly political set of questions.

The emergence of risk society is highly relevant to Tony Blair's project for New Labour. Blair is often spoken of as a conservative, who is destroying the values and perspectives of the left. I think it could be said, on the contrary, that he is one of the few leading politicians who is actively trying to come to terms with the profound changes affecting local life and the global order. In that sense, his orientation could fairly be described as a radical one. However, the arrival of risk society means that the idea of modernization, which Blair treats as central, needs to be rethought.

Modernization, as Blair uses the term, means bringing Britain up to date. Tony Blair has been the archetypical modernizer within the Labour Party; but more fundamentally, he wants to modernize British institutions – modernization carrying the connotation in this country that Britain lags behind other industrial societies in various key respects. Now this is a bit like the first explanation that Sebag Montefiore mentions for the collapse of Barings Bank – crusty old institutions which have lost their relevance to the modern world.

That there is something in the project of modernization, thus understood, can be seen by anyone who sets foot in the House of Lords. In risk society, however, modernization means something different. Risk society is industrial society which has come up against its own limitations, where those limitations take the form of manufactured risk. Modernization in this sense, cannot simply be 'more of the same'.

We should distinguish here between simple and reflexive modernization. Simple modernization is old-type unilinear modernization; reflexive modernization, by contrast, implies coming to terms with the limits and contradictions of the modern order. These are obvious in new domains of politics associated with various sorts of social movements. They are obvious in motorway protests, in animal rights demonstrations and in many of the food scares. Second-phase modernization – modernization as reflexive modernization – will not look like first-phase modernization. There is an opportunity, I think, for political debate in this country to leap ahead of many other European countries in this respect and I would like to see this happen. Reflexive modernization, like risk more generally, is by no means wholly a negative prospect and offers many possibilities for positive political engagement.

Our relationship to science and technology today is different from that characteristic of early industrial society. In Western society, for some two centuries, science functioned as a sort of tradition. Scientific knowledge was supposed to overcome tradition but actually became a taken-for-granted authority in its own right. It was something which most people respected, but was external to their lives. Lay people 'took' opinions from the experts.

The more science and technology intrude into our lives, the less this external perspective holds. Most of us – including government authorities and politicians – have, and have to have, a much more dialogic or engaged relationship with science and technology than used to be the case. We cannot simply 'accept' the findings which scientists produce, if only because scientists so frequently disagree with one another, particularly in situations of manufactured risk. And everyone now recognizes the essentially sceptical character of science described earlier. Whenever someone decides what to eat, what to have for breakfast, whether to drink decaffeinated or ordinary coffee, that person takes a decision in the context of conflicting, changeable scientific and technological information.

There is no way out of this situation – we are all caught up in it, even if we choose to proceed 'as if in ignorance'. Politics must give some institutional form to this dialogical engagement because at the moment it concerns only special interest groups, who mostly struggle outside the main political domain. We do not currently possess institutions which allow us to monitor technological change. We might have prevented the BSE debacle if a public dialogue had already been established about technological change and its problematic consequences. Enoch Powell apparently remarked that nothing affects our lives as much as technological change and he was right – yet such change is completely outside the democratic system. More public means of engaging with science and technology wouldn't do away with the quandary of scaremongering versus cover-ups, but it might allow us to mute some of its more damaging consequences.

These considerations are relevant to rethinking the welfare state. The welfare state was founded against the backdrop of a society where nature was still nature and tradition was still tradition. This is obvious, for example, in the gender provisions in the post-1945 welfare state, which simply presumed the continuity of the 'traditional family'. It is obvious in terms of the growth of the National Health Service, which was set up as a response mechanism to illness understood as external risk.

In a world of more active engagement with health, with the body, with marriage, with gender, with work – in an era of manufactured risk – the welfare state cannot continue on in the form in which it developed in the post-1945 settlement. The crisis of the welfare state is not purely fiscal, it is a crisis of risk management in a society dominated by a new type of risk.

These observations are relevant to class division. J. K. Galbraith's so-called 'culture of contentment' was a bit of a shooting star – there is no culture of contentment. One reason why many middle-class and professional groups have opted out of public welfare schemes is bound up with a certain attitude towards risk management. In risk society, the middle classes detach themselves from public provision and in a certain sense they are right to do so because that provision was geared to a different interpretation and situation of risk. When people have a more active orientation to their lives, they also have to have a more active orientation to risk management, so it is not surprising that those who can afford it tend to opt out of existing welfare systems.

Political debate in Britain needs to take much greater account of the significance of ecological debates, themselves deeply bound up with the advance of manufactured risk. Ecological questions precisely reflect a world living after nature and after tradition. Many forms of lifestyle politics develop which have no precedent in the earlier type of industrial society. Protesters some while ago made a great deal of fuss about veal calves being transported to the continent in constrained and artificial conditions. Their critics called them sentimental. Yet in the light of the experience of BSE, everyone can see that this wasn't just sentiment. The protests reflected a latent sense of what can happen when the industrial production of food becomes distanced from nature – or what used to be nature. A moral commitment to animal rights is, in a certain sense, a hard-edged politics – after all, even measured in narrow economic terms, the BSE crisis has been a disaster. Calculations put the cost to the British economy at £6 billion or perhaps even more.

Risk society is not the same as postmodernism. Postmodern interpretations see politics as at an end – political power simply loses its significance with the passing of modernity. Yet modernity does not disappear with the arrival of manufactured risk; rather modernization, which continues, takes on new meanings and subtleties. Reflexive modernization presumes and generates a politics. That politics cannot unfold completely outside the parliamentary domain. Social movements and special interest groups cannot supply what parliamentary politics offers – the means of reconciling different interests with one another, and also of balancing different risks in relation to one another. The issues I have discussed demand to be brought more directly into the political arena. A party able to address them cogently would be in a prime position in the political encounters that will unfold over the coming few years.

3

Lessons of Lloyd's: the Limits of Insurance

ADAM RAPHAEL

Insurance is meant to be about the spreading of risk rather than its concentration. The folly of the Lloyd's underwriters, who ignored this age-old principle, lost investors to the market more than £10 billion in five years. No British financial institution has ever lost so much money and survived. As such, there must still be a question mark over the future of Lloyd's.

Reflecting on whether I am more likely to be struck down by lightning, mad-cow disease or perhaps struck dumb, I realize that it is by far my most likely fate to be struck down by a dispatch rider as I jaywalk across Pall Mall. That is the trouble with risk, few of us are much good at assessing it. That is particularly true about the 15,000 fools, idiots, speculators, naive, call them what you will, among whom I include myself, who thought it would be a good idea to invest in the Lloyd's insurance market in the 1980s. There were even some quite sharp characters who did so, businessmen, merchant bankers, lawyers, even insurance brokers, who decided to try their luck. But most of those who became names at Lloyd's during this period were financial innocents from country vicarages, farmers, ex-soldiers, even the odd widow or discarded wife who was generously given membership of Lloyd's as part of the divorce settlement.

It seemed a safe bet at the time. Here was an institution which had traded profitably for more than three hundred years, a pillar of the City of London, its standard was *uberima fides*, 'utmost good faith', and it prided itself on the highest standards of integrity etc. Of course you traded on the basis of unlimited liability, but so of course do all sole traders. The difference with Lloyd's is that you place your entire wealth in the hands of an underwriter who may or may not be competent, may or may not be drunk and may or may not be crooked. Looking back on it, the idea of placing your fate in the hands of people you don't know, in a business you can't understand, and where the risks are totally opaque, but potentially huge, was madness of a high order. But many thousands of us did, gulled by the history and traditions of the market, by the smooth talk of members' agents and by our own folly.

In some cases there was also outright deception and near fraud, which is why the names, as the investors are called, win most of the cases that come before the courts. One of the things one quickly learns as a Lloyd's name is that public sympathy is strictly limited. Max Hastings, formerly of the *Telegraph* now editor of the *Evening Standard*, brilliantly summed up the public mood of *schadenfreude* when he congratulated himself on not being so foolish as to join. 'Whenever life', he wrote in the *Spectator*, 'has looked a little glum in the last year or two, I have been able to console myself with the reflection that I am not a member of Lloyd's. Once upon a time, smug fat men sidled up to one on shoots and smirked horribly "just got the Lloyd's cheque, very nice number, pays for the wife to go to Portugal with her boyfriend, settles the school fees, takes care of the cartridges, you really ought to think about it."'

But of course, for every smug shooter that Max knows, there are people like Betty Atkins and Bridget Milling-Smith whom I met over the past two or three years while researching my book *Ultimate Risk*.[1] Betty Atkins was a secretary at Lloyd's who had worked in a broking firm for over thirty-five years; as a retirement present the broker said to her and to another secretary in the office, 'We'll make you names at Lloyd's, don't worry we'll provide a bank guarantee, we'll take out stop loss insurance, it's all going to be wonderful and it will provide you with a nice retirement nest egg.' Of course it has turned out to be an absolute total disaster for Betty Atkins. The guarantee vanished into thin air, the stop loss proved to be defective and the broker forgot about the promises that were made to her and she is now ruined. She has lost her house, lost everything and had a nightmarish period, perhaps even worse than her financial problems. It has affected her whole life over the past four years.

Bridget Milling-Smith was the widow of an SAS officer who was killed in Oman. She came back to the UK and was persuaded by some commercial bankers to gamble with Lloyd's, since she would need help to educate her children privately. The only wealth she had were investments totalling about £60–70,000 and a small cottage. The result again was total ruin. 'Don't worry your pretty little head,' she was told at one point when she raised some concerns about the nature of risk at Lloyd's.

So how did it all go so wrong? Insurance is about assessing, quantifying and above all spreading risk. Simply put, Lloyd's failed in these most basic of tasks. An underwriter is not unlike a track-side bookie at a horse race meeting. He needs to balance his books, he needs to assess the risk of any eventuality and if there is too much money on the favourite, he should lay off some of the incoming bets with another bookie via a frantic piece of tick-tacking across the market. Underwriting is no different from that bookie's operations. The *New Statesman* once accurately described Lloyd's as a 'mob of upper-class bookies with a mild talent for PR'. The trouble is that many underwriters were not nearly as bright or as numerate as your average bookie. Insurance is not about the acceptance of risk, but its management. In the words of a 1601 Elizabethan statute, 'the loss lighteth rather easily upon many than heavily upon few.' The problem was that Lloyd's and its underwriters forgot these basic tenets. If they hadn't done so they wouldn't have lost so much money. The scale of Lloyd's losses is really extraordinary: £10 billion in five years. 'No British institution has ever lost so much money and survived': those are not my words but those of the former chief executive Peter Middleton. The question is whether Lloyd's can survive or will be dragged down by its past errors.

The trigger to the Lloyd's disaster was its failure to manage capacity. Between 1983 and 1988 the market's capital base doubled at an average growth rate of more than 15 per cent annually at a time when premiums grew by only 3 per cent. Fuelling this huge expansion, the number of names also doubled in those years. Irresponsibility characterized this whole period. In the 1960s, before you were allowed to trade at Lloyd's, you had to have minimum standards of wealth and you were not allowed to use your house as evidence of your wealth. However, throughout the 1970s and 1980s Lloyd's continually lowered the standards of entry. A person showing wealth of less than £70,000, sometimes as low as £37,500, secured against the guarantee of their main house, could become a name. This of course attracted lots of characters, with totally inadequate resources, to enter into a risk market. Those most responsible at Lloyd's must have realized that by undermining their own standards they were going to attract many people into the market who would be destroyed by just one or two years' losses. The authorities at Lloyd's carry a heavy responsibility for what then happened. Many people gambled their houses and lost them or are now in the process of losing them.

The nature of the insurance cycle has been the same since time immemorial. It is not unlike other markets in that when times are good, when premiums are high and rates are good, underwriters make money. Money then flows into the market and rates begin to soften, losses begin to be incurred and, with a bit of pain and hardship, money flows out of the market. And so the cycle begins again: rates harden and premiums go up and people start making money. Like any other market, Lloyd's is prone to excess. Yet there has never been quite such a bubble as that which happened at Lloyd's over the last five years. Interestingly, Lloyd's was founded just after the South Sea Bubble in the eighteenth century and what has happened in the past few years certainly is a classic bubble.

One of the most disastrous consequences of the excess capacity that flowed into the market during the 1980s was that it fuelled the LMX spiral. Just to describe the LMX spiral took many pages of the book and rather defeats me even now, but I shall try to explain. Imagine that insurance is like a multilevelled cake, a huge cake that goes up in tiers. Insurers take particular layers of the cake to insure. But in the 1980s, as the risks on some of these projects got larger and larger, on an oil well, or a North Sea platform, the multitiered insurance had to be used sequentially to cover these particular risks. For example, a group of marine underwriters at Lloyd's who were not securing enough premium from their traditional marine market decided to venture into this arena of excess loss insurance. This entails covering a risk above a certain level, so that maybe underwriter A would cover the first £5 million, underwriter B would cover the next £5 million and underwriter C would cover the next £10 million. But these underwriters added a different twist to this particular form of reinsurance – they began to reinsure one another – so you had A reinsuring B who reinsured C who reinsured back into A who reinsured back into B and so it went on.

This was wonderful for the brokers because they creamed off 10 per cent commission each time one of these reinsurances was placed within the market. The problem with this practice was that the risk became more and more opaque. By the time the spiral had gone round two or three times, not even Isaac Newton would have been able to determine what risk was actually being carried. So when a series of natural catastrophes occurred – as happened in the 1980s with Hurricane Hugo and others – the spiral began to unwind, claims were made and huge losses were made by a few irresponsible underwriters. A High Court judge commented that one underwriter 'did his incompetent best'. There is no doubt about it, some underwriters were near fraudulent, but most of them were just totally incompetent. The risks were not discernible, not knowable by anyone and they reached a point where the underwriters were just playing with other people's fortunes. The result was predictable: the spiral was hit and huge sums were lost.

Yet we cannot completely understand what was happening by just blaming a few incompetents in the market. This huge expansion served the interests of a number of professionals in the market as they secured their livelihoods by large commissions. The brokers certainly benefited, as I have described, by taking commissions on the reinsurance. But so also did the members and the managing agents who work on a basis of profit commission. The more they expanded, the more commission amassed. This was particularly important in the late 1970s and 1980s when many of them wanted to capitalize their businesses and get out. The more profit they were able to show, the more likely they were to be able to sell out, and so a huge conflict of interest arose within the market.

Lloyd's really only worked as well as it did for hundreds of years because the interests were relatively aligned. Although the underwriter and the names were often friends and it was a very cosy, closed little world, it is of course in the nature of markets everywhere that the insiders always do better. But at least the insiders had some regard for the names, the investors and the outsiders who were backing them. In the 1980s these relationships broke down. There were just too many people in the market, too many people who were greedy and too many conflicts of interest which in the end resulted in disaster.

Another odd aspect of Lloyd's is that it works on the basis of an *annual trading venture*. This practice goes back to the early days of the eighteenth century when ships were insured. Each year is unique and the profits and losses of that year are decided at the end of a three-year period: the length of time it took for the ships to get back to port. To make sense of an annual trading venture of this kind, it needs to be understood that since many of the risks stretch beyond a year's period or even beyond a three-year period, those risks have to be rolled over by a syndicate. Every year, the syndicate reinsures those risks to a new syndicate venture, often of the same people. This is a rollover of all the risks, so that latent risks, such as asbestos and pollution which I shall come on to very briefly, were rolled over when the outcome was not known. This requires enormous integrity from the people who are actually doing that reinsurance because the profit and loss on any one year depends on the amount that is paid for reinsurance. With the conflicts of interests that arose in the market, some of these reinsurances were near fraudulent.

The impact of asbestos and pollution added to the risk equation. Asbestos was a well-known risk throughout the early part of this century but Lloyd's, unlike most American insurers, went on insuring American corporations against asbestos risk right through the 1940s and 1950s and indeed into the 1960s. They also reinsured them on policies which were very open ended and which did not limit the risk in the way that they should have done. When the American judiciary decided to extend liability under these asbestos insurances in the 1970s, Lloyd's was desperately exposed and the potential liabilities are still substantial. It is still uncertain whether Lloyd's will be able to survive these liabilities. It is also uncertain how many people are going to die from asbestos in the next thirty years in the USA and the UK, but it could run into tens of thousands. The exposures are already there, it is just a question of when they impact.

Pollution is a different horror story. When the US Congress, in its wisdom, passed the Super Fund reforms of the 1980s in an attempt to clear up corporate America, most of the reinsurances on environmental pollution were placed at Lloyd's. Many of them were certainly disproportionate and that again has cost the market billions. It is only congressional action that can clear up this particular situation, because the liabilities are so huge. At one time the pollution liabilities were estimated at a trillion dollars. They have since reduced, but are still enormous and probably more than the capacity of the companies who reinsured these risks. At present, there are various reform proposals before Congress, which may or may not be enacted.

The final variable that undoubtedly changed the risk/reward ratio was the advent of the Conservative government and low taxation policies. Lloyd's had benefited enormously from Labour governments with marginal rates of taxation of 98 per cent. When losses were made in the market in the 1970s, they were borne largely by the taxpayer. With a loss of, say, £20,000 in a single year, made by someone paying tax at the highest rate, in theory the amount they actually lost was only 2 per cent of the £20,000, that is £400. At the low marginal rates of taxation in the Thatcher period, the risk/reward ratio at Lloyd's changed, so that when losses were made they were substantial.

So the old Lloyd's has gone. There is no doubt about it, it is finished, it is over. The idea of unlimited liability borne by individuals has gone for all time. The question is, can the market survive in any form at all, and if it does, what form does it take? Clearly the likely form is a corporate market much more like the insurance companies in the City of London and elsewhere. The old buccaneering days of individual underwriters backed by a hundred names have gone for good. Lloyd's is just one of those British institutions which was flawed, which survived when it was a very closed small world: as soon as it expanded, conflicts of interest arose between the professionals who were underwriting and those they were underwriting for. Inevitably, at some point in time there was going to be a crash, but quite the size of the crash has, I think, stunned most of the market professionals and has at least given them pause for thought as to how they pursue their business in future.

Note

1 Adam Raphael, *Ultimate Risk* (Bantam, London, 1995).

4

Nature Bites Back

JOHN GRAY

The current crisis over the safety of British beef occurs within a month of the tenth anniversary of the explosions at Chernobyl. The two meltdowns that occurred on 26 April 1986 at the Chernobyl nuclear power station, seventy-two miles from the Ukrainian capital of Kiev, created a mile-high plume of radio-active gas and particles whose fall-out was felt in countries as distant as Sweden and Greece. A large area around Chernobyl remains deserted and will be uninhabitable for several centuries.

The long-term effects of this fall-out on human health and the natural environment are still not precisely calculable though they are undoubtedly highly significant. Official Soviet attempts to play down their seriousness were a key factor in fuelling the demands for glasnost and for Ukrainian independence, which triggered the collapse of the Soviet Union itself.

The public health crisis that may result from links between BSE and Creutzfeldt-Jakob disease (CJD) in humans has repercussions and implications as profound as those of Chernobyl. It forces us to reconsider the culture of technological mastery of nature that we inherit from earlier ages. It compels us to question whether it is wise to go on treating nature – the Earth, other species and even our human genetic inheritance – as merely a pool of resources to be exploited in the service of our present wants. Is it any longer acceptable that whenever evidence surfaces of the riskiness of our interventions in natural processes, governments should consistently err on the side of technological optimism? Is there not now an overwhelming case for a genuinely conservative policy – one guided by prudence and respect for nature rather than groundless confidence in the powers of technology?

There can be little doubt that some of the responsibility for the BSE crisis at the end of the 1990s falls on Thatcherite policies of deregulation which, for much of the 1980s, allowed cattle to be fed meat rendered from sheep contaminated by scrapie. New Right policies rank long-term considerations of public health and the integrity of the environment a long way behind present risks to commercial profit. The immense power of the farming and food lobbies in Britain meant that neoliberal policies here in the 1980s were bound to favour producer interests over public safety. In many ways, the government's predicament was a direct result of a fatal combination of the power of those producer lobbies with an anti-government ideology committed to minimizing environmental risk.

New Right thought scoffed at concern for the environment, denied the ecological responsibilities of government and aimed to privatize environmental risk by transferring responsibility to the market. In such a climate it was easy to confuse risks that are unquantifiable with risks that are insignificant. The risk to human health posed by the transmission of disease-bearing pathogens across animal species to the human species was not, and is not, exactly quantifiable; but given the enormity of the danger posed by the possibility of an epidemic of CJD, it is not at all insignificant. During the Thatcher period a policy of prudence, aiming to avoid or minimize such incalculable but catastrophic risks, never stood a chance of being adopted.

The present threat to public health is probably only one of many malign inheritances of the 1980s that we will have to cope with in the coming years. It would nevertheless be a mistake to think that responsibility for the environmental dangers we are facing lies only with Thatcherism. A larger threat to human health arises from the hyperindustrialization of farming and from the technological hubris which pervades our entire culture. Farming today is an industry at the cutting edge of technological intervention in natural processes. It embodies, more even than much traditional manufacturing industry, the modern belief that the Earth is made up of raw materials for human technological ingenuity to work on.

Did it not occur to anyone that feeding animal protein to what nature has evolved to be a herbivorous species might be dangerous? Yet even such an act of folly is less hubristic than policies for the genetic engineering of animal species that are now on the scientific and commercial agenda. The industrialization of farming is only an incident in a much grander project of subduing nature to human designs. Is it altogether fanciful to see the threat of a major outbreak of CJD as a symptom of nature's rebellion against human hubris?

Much of our culture is still animated by the anthropocentric belief that the human species is independent of nature. This belief is at the root of some of the most admirable modern achievements. We have eradicated some infectious diseases and, in parts of the world, we have eliminated starvation and the worst forms of destitution. These successes have encouraged the expectation that the natural limits placed on us by scarcity and mortality can be progressively overcome. They support the conviction that there is no human problem that is not soluble by technological ingenuity.

There are many signs that such hopes are hubristic. Tuberculosis and other infectious diseases are returning in forms that are highly resistant to antibiotics. Male fertility has been declining, apparently as a consequence of changes we have made but not begun to understand in our everyday environment. The pursuit of intensive agriculture through the development of high-yielding crops has produced monocultures that are exceptionally vulnerable to disease. In these and other examples, the modern project of constructing a technosphere in which the human species is freed from dependency on the Earth is coming up against limits imposed by nature. It is as if the Earth itself were resisting our attempt to transform it into an adjunct of human purposes.

We cannot undo the technological progress of the past several centuries. Nor should we attempt to do so, since practically everything that is worthwhile in modern societies comes from people no longer having to live on the edge of subsistence – an achievement that only technological advance has made possible. The lesson to be drawn from the prospect of a CJD epidemic is not

Luddism. It is that we must have more respect for the natural world on which we depend, and invest fewer of our hopes in the project of transforming it by the use of technology. Farming practices which treat animals not as living creatures but as assemblages of manipulable genes and proteins must be reformed. Projects of genetic engineering that propose to alter species – including the human species – for the sake of commercial or even humanitarian benefit must be viewed with suspicion. The potential benefits of new technologies must always be weighed against their risks. We should be ready to err on the side of caution.

A genuinely conservative policy of this kind goes against the grain of much that is good in our culture. It is easily caricatured as unreasonably risk-averse. The evidence of recent history suggests that it is technological utopianism that is unreasonable. Unless we moderate our hopes of technology, the disasters of the past decade will be repeated, perhaps on a grander scale. It would be a sad commentary on the human capacity for learning from mistakes if, ten years after Chernobyl, we were to fail to grasp the warning against human hubris presented by that disaster – and the one that may be unfolding in Britain.

5

Risky Business, Safety

MARTIN WOOLLACOTT

That we should be reduced to animal sacrifice at the end of the twentieth century was not expected. Yet that is what is happening when a British government explains that it is contemplating the mass slaughter of cattle not on scientific grounds but to restore public confidence. That the action, if it is taken, is highly unlikely to do so adds to the surreal nature of the exercise.

The extraordinary logic of doing something which you have explained in advance is not necessary represents a lurch into the realm of superstition. Like a Roman worshipper hesitating between temples, the government was thinking only in terms of propitiation. There could not be clearer evidence that the ruling party in Britain still did not understand a profound shift in modern politics which has displaced wealth creation and military security, narrowly conceived, as the main aims and justification for government. That shift has made the avoidance of the dangers arising from society's own economic and technological development not just one of government's responsibilities but its main business.

This transition to what Ulrich Beck has called 'risk society' dethrones both the deities, Science and Public Opinion, to which Mr Major appeals, or more accurately, of which at the moment he sees himself the victim. It means that effective governments have to understand that they preside over societies which have become laboratories of technological and social change, in which dependence on technology must go hand in hand with control of technology.

Dependence and control cannot be separated in time. Nor can decisions over those risks be taken, Beck argues, by the old alliance between scientists, industry and secretive government, but only by open governments, by much better informed publics, and by socially aware firms and economic institutions – all of them brought face to face with consequences from which they are at present largely divorced. Speaking at a well-timed conference on the Politics of Risk Society organized by the Institute for Public Policy Research, Professor Beck said that the lives of the British have become 'an experiment inflicted upon us by the beef industry'. The situation of being in an uncontrolled, unintended and unstoppable experiment arose when old and inadequate methods of risk assessment prevailed. But the arguments of Ulrich Beck, like those of Anthony Giddens, do not pretend that risk can be banished from modern life.

Indeed, they argue that risk *characterizes* modern societies, and that the control of risk represents a kind of second wave of modernization. Giddens, speaking at the same conference, suggested that both major British political parties have been involved in different versions of an earlier kind of modernization, of bringing Britain 'up to date'. The Conservatives, he implied, were still stuck in what was now an obsolete and even a dangerous project. Labour had a clearer view of the need for a transition but had not yet made it.

Critics of such ideas have pointed out that modern industrial societies are much less dangerous than earlier ones. Individuals in the rich world live out their lives in much greater safety than in previous generations. One response is that certain kinds of disasters – nuclear breakdowns, global warming – could change that happy picture. The other is that, as far as lesser dangers are concerned, the point is that we have far higher expectations of control and are far more responsible for the dangers we face than in the past. In the main, we manufacture our own disasters. Beck expresses this by saying that modern politics is about the 'distribution of bads' rather than the distribution of goods. Giddens insists that every time we assess risks we are acting politically, assigning values and choosing between them.

Useful ideas, at a time when risk continues to be assessed by different professional orders who then measure it on the basis of their different professional yardsticks. The central insight of the risk society concept is that industrial societies both manufacture and must control risk. Risks are not just moments of danger as we forge forward: they are the process itself. Managing this process is, or ought to be, the dominant concern of their government. It is what their publics expect of them, as the Conservatives are learning, or re-learning, at the moment. The generalized association of government with the avoidance of risk, or with compensation for it when it arises, is deeply rooted, in all classes, and among people of all political views.

It is also true that the public punishes overcaution as well as lack of caution. It does not want to pay a high price for avoiding risks which turn out not to be real. But if governments want peoples who are more understanding, they have to associate them, more directly and continuously, with the decisions which lead to risks being taken. Effective risk prevention cannot emerge out of the haphazard interaction between a science which will always hold out against absolute conclusions, an industry maximizing production and profit, and a public opinion veering between greed and fear. Nor can the complexity of the decisions be reduced to a simple equation, with environmental consequences on the one hand and economic advantage on the other. The question must rather be: what kind of risks are we prepared to take in order to be the society we want to be?

6

Risk Society, Politics and BSE

ROBIN GROVE-WHITE

The BSE crisis is a crisis for our politics as much as for public health. It signals a new stage in the tangled relationships between science, 'the environment', and modern government.

Further environmental time-bombs are ticking away in the undergrowth. The implications for our patterns of political authority are deep and troubling. So far, the Labour leadership, like that of the Conservative government itself, has focused only on the short-term political implications of the issue.

However there is now a growing body of social thought on the ways in which the culture and priorities of modern industrial societies are leading to a continuous intensification of risks for all of us – the 'risk society' thesis.

Social analysts like Ulrich Beck and Anthony Giddens highlight the ways in which apparent strengths of modern society – the reliance on perpetual industrial innovation, our reductionist 'scientific' approaches to evaluating such innovations, and the growing 'individualization' of our personal identities – are generating new patterns of political anxiety and conflict around major risk issues. Yet the full contours of such conflicts continue to be largely unacknowledged by orthodox political parties and institutions.

The mounting reliance of everyone in modern society on the judgements of 'experts' is paralleled by the growing ability of many of us, reinforced by modern media, to deconstruct political reassurance couched as scientific or technical 'fact'. This has been the classic pattern in environmental controversies over the past two decades, about nuclear power, motorways, animal welfare, disposal of oil platforms in the North Sea such as the Brent Spar, and so on.

The current BSE alarms reflect crucial features of these new patterns of risk crisis, in a British context. In the immediate furore, and in a universal anxiety to establish a bedrock of certainty in which to locate trust, there has been an intensified focus on 'the experts' – in this case, the scientists studying cause–effect relationships between BSE in cattle and CJD in humans. Predictably, given the alarming stakes for public health, the political exchanges and media witch-hunts have followed ritual patterns: allegations of political neglect and bad faith, reflecting a large measure of hindsight in relation to what 'the scientists' have been telling us.

But there is a deeper, more troubling issue for the future. Is science fitted for the role of arbiter of what is or is not to be held acceptable in the field of industrial innovation? If not, what alternatives are there? Repeatedly over the past ten years, ministers have asserted the non-existence of 'evidence' or 'proof' of a precise causal connection between BSE and CJD as the justification for limited action. What's more, notwithstanding the healthily contrary views of Professor Lacey and other dissidents, they may well have been justified in doing so. The state of sure knowledge of patterns of BSE cause and effect has indeed been limited – primarily because it is only recently that scientists have begun searching systematically for any such patterns.

But this is *normal* in science. Contrary to the still-dominant myth in Western culture, science does not offer an unambiguous baseline of fact about our surroundings. Characteristically, its processes are far more socially shaped, more tentative, indeed more creative. Scientific investigation may tell us about specified relationships – but only if those guiding it are able first to pose the precise questions. Moreover, recent changes in the world of university funding and technology foresight are tending to narrow the focus of research to conform to what established interests deem useful.

So at one level, in their assertions of 'no proof' in the BSE/CJD domain, ministers are reflecting reality. But at the same time they have sought to hide behind the misguided myth of the normative intellectual authority of scientific knowledge in our culture.

Understandably, scientists have not resisted such elevation of their influence. They have established an increasingly uncomfortable *mariage de convenance* with modern government. The resulting coalition is perpetuating unrealistically inflated expectations of the social authority of the (in other respects valuable) knowledge scientists generate.

Hence, our own version of the risk society has emerged. Industrial innovation plunges ahead in areas of relative scientific ignorance. Regulators and ministerial advisory committees stumble along behind, discovering by trial and error the implicit pitfalls, seeking to contain and mitigate them. Meanwhile, ministers lean on the absence of conclusive proof or evidence of harm, and the inherited (but increasingly brittle) social authority of a particular positivistic view of science, to keep the show on the road. We have seen this again and again, with pesticides, with low-level radiation, with the impacts of the motor car.

The perils of such patterns are now stark. Consider the new arena of biotechnology, where industrial innovation is already well ahead of the capacity of regulators to assess or control the full potential implications of releases of genetically modified organisms (GMO) into the wider environment. GMO regulators focus only a relatively restricted range of parameters driven by existing limited scientific knowledge, while sidelining wider moral and ecological factors. Anxieties about these patterns, articulated by environmental groups, rogue scientists and other individuals, are patronized by ministers and their advisers as unsupported by proof, much as in the BSE case.

There is a host of similar issues now in the pipeline. Possible links between oestrogen and declining male fertility and worries about cancer risks from omnipresent overhead power lines are just two of the most conspicuous. But the crucial point is, *we simply do not know what is out there.*

So how can our politics handle the roller-coaster of risk innovation less capriciously than present arrangements allow? To abandon key social decisions on patterns of all-encompassing technological change to the judgements of small groups of scientists would simply compound the problems, intensifying scepticism about scientific reassurance when things go wrong, and further corroding the authority of governments.

The only way forward to contain future crises of this sort is through a franker *shared* sense of the new forms of uncertainty in which we are all now increasingly embedded in advanced industrial society, and wider genuine participation in the far-reaching *social* judgements (do we or do we not feel comfortable about feeding ruminants with other diseased ruminants?) to be made under such conditions of chronic indeterminacy. This calls for radical new thinking about institutional reform, a path along which even the Labour and Liberal Democrat parties have barely begun to advance.

7

Procrastination, Precaution and the Global Gamble

STEPHEN TINDALE

Of all the myriad risks facing the individual at the end of the twentieth century, environmental risks are among the most pervasive, the most serious and the most feared. They are also in some respects new: what Anthony Giddens has described as 'manufactured risk'. The risk of disease has always been with us; the risk of unemployment has been more or less prevalent since the enclosure of the commons drove subsistence peasants off the land. The risks surrounding nuclear power or biotechnology, in contrast, are factors which were unknown to previous generations. Indeed, as the risk of imminent war has receded in the developed world, and as some diseases have been controlled, so environmental concerns have moved up the psychological agenda.

This is not to say that the concept of environmental threat is new. Whole civilizations have been destroyed by environmental change. The Harappa culture which flourished in the Indus valley 3,500 to 4,500 years ago was destroyed by a combination of deforestation, loss of topsoil and a change in the micro-climate.[1] The Icelandic society chronicled in the Sagas was virtually wiped out by the 'Little Ice Age' which lasted from the fourteenth to the eighteenth century. But since the Enlightenment and the scientific advances which resulted, environmental threats have been regarded by the dominant, technologically based ideology as having been solved. Nature had been tamed.

Ecologists are highly critical of modern science, which is seen as exploitative and destructive. For example, the American physicist Fritjof Capra writes as follows:

> The medieval outlook changed radically in the sixteenth and seventeenth centuries. The notion of an organic, living and spiritual universe was replaced by that of the world as a machine ... This development was brought about by revolutionary changes in physics and astronomy, culminating in the achievements of Copernicus, Galileo and Newton. The science of the seventeenth century was based on a new method of enquiry, advocated forcefully by Francis Bacon, which involved the mathematical description of nature and the analytical method of reasoning. The Baconian spirit profoundly changed the nature and purpose of the scientific quest. From the time of the ancients the goals of science had been wisdom, understanding the natural order and living in harmony with it ... In the seventeenth century this attitude changed to its polar opposite, from integration to self-assertion. Since Bacon, the goal of science has been knowledge that can be used to dominate and control nature.[2]

The link between the domination of external nature and the domination of internal human nature was central to the thinking of the early Frankfurt School. Adorno and Horkheimer, condemning the Baconian determination 'to enable Man to hold sway over a disenchanted nature', argue that the instrumental rationality which leads us to suppress the aesthetic, expressive and instinctive rationalities within ourselves leads us too to exploit the natural world.[3] 'Critical theory's observation [is] that it is the spread of a certain form of Enlightenment rationality to all areas and most parts of conscious existence that underpins our exploitative relationship with the natural world.'[4]

This instrumental view of nature's place, one of the most pervasive parts of the Enlightenment inheritance, leads some ecologists to reject the Enlightenment altogether. This is well expressed in the following extract by the Indian writer Vandana Shiva:

> The Age of Enlightenment, and the theory of progress to which it gave rise, was centred on the sacredness of two categories: modern scientific knowledge and economic development. Somewhere along

the way, the unbridled pursuit of progress, guided by science and development, began to destroy life without any assessment of how fast and how much the diversity of life on this planet is disappearing. The act of living and conserving life in all its diversity – in people and in nature – seems to have been sacrificed to progress, and the sanctity of life been substituted by the sanctity of science and development. Throughout the world, a new questioning is growing, rooted in the experience of those for whom the spread of what is called 'Enlightenment' has been the spread of darkness.[5]

This new questioning – the undermining of the sanctity of science – can be attributed in part to a realization that the Baconian promise was false. Nature has not been tamed, and is increasingly rebellious in the face of technological oppression. The agricultural innovations which were intended to banish famine degrade the land and poison the waters. The urban industrial society which was thought to insulate humans from natural catastrophe is itself threatening, through global warming, to cause more serious floods, droughts and storms. While the pre-Enlightenment consciousness regarded environmental risks as natural and unavoidable, the work of God or other unknown forces, the post-Enlightenment consciousness recognizes that some of them are manufactured.

Questioning science – the precautionary principle

Modern environmental policy, in theory at least, recognizes the limits to the predictive powers of science. Most public authorities are rhetorically committed to the 'precautionary principle', which Jordan and O'Riordan have defined as 'giving the environment the benefit of any reasonable doubt' and 'shifting the burden of proof from the victim to the developer'.[6] Both the European Union and the British government have signed up to this concept. The EU does not define it, though it is written into the Maastricht Treaty. The British government has given the following explanation:

> We must act on facts, and on the most accurate interpretation of them, using the best scientific and economic information. That does not mean we must sit back until we have one hundred per cent evidence about everything. Where the state of our planet is at stake, the risks can be so high and the costs of corrective action so great,

that prevention is better and cheaper than cure. We must analyse the possible benefits and costs both of action and of inaction. Where there are significant risks of damage to the environment, the Government will be prepared to take precautionary action to limit the use of potentially dangerous materials or the spread of potentially damaging pollutants, even where scientific knowledge is not conclusive, if the balance of likely costs and benefits justifies it.[7]

A good example of the limits of the predictive power of science is the way in which CFCs were hailed as wonder chemicals when first produced in bulk in the 1920s. They were non-toxic – good news for industrial workers – non-flammable and highly stable. But this very stability was the cause of the problem, because they are not broken down until they reach the upper atmosphere and are destroyed by the intensity of the sun's rays. So chlorine is released into the stratosphere, paving the way for the catalytic reactions which destroy ozone. Nobody predicted this until the 1970s, and it was not generally accepted until after an ozone hole had been detected over Antarctica in the 1980s.

Precaution in practice

There are, however, some cases where public policy does operate on the basis of the precautionary principle. With new medicines, or substances likely to enter the human food chain, for example, the burden of proof is very clearly with the developer. The developer has to subject the new product to a stringent set of toxicity tests to prove that it is safe – these can cost up to half a million pounds. It has to be demonstrated that any toxicity is below the 'no observed effect level'. If there are observable effects, the product will not be passed, even if the link of causation cannot be explained.[8]

Two specific instances of precaution in practice are the EU's approach to pesticides in drinking water and the use of animal growth hormones. The maximum permissible level for pesticides in drinking water is 0.1 micrograms per litre – which effectively means zero. There is thought to be strong public support for the notion of pesticide-free drinking water – Friends of the Earth ran a campaign some years ago asking 'do you want weedkiller in your water?' But there is no toxicological evidence to justify such a low limit. The cost of meeting it is extremely high. The Drinking Water Directive therefore fails a conventional cost–benefit analysis, and the UK government is arguing within the EU for a relaxation. The European Commission proposes to retain the current standard. A House of Lords Select Committee report backs the Commission:

> There are strong political reasons for maintaining the standard irrespective of public health considerations. However, on public health grounds too the standard should remain in force: the uncertainty about the possible effects of pesticide mixtures and of the products of pesticide breakdown . . . is such that the precautionary principle justifies the Commission's proposal.[9]

In the case of animal growth hormones, a group of experts advised the European Commission that three such products were safe provided that certain conditions of use were observed: these included specific dose limits, non-edible sites of injection, full veterinary supervision and a minimum waiting period before sale of treated meat. The European Council of Ministers – under intense pressure from certain political interests – rejected this advice and banned the hormones. Whatever the true motive for the Council's decision, it is clearly possible to argue that such stringent conditions would be unlikely to be observed in all cases on all farms across Western Europe, and that the hormones should therefore be banned as a precaution.[10]

The furore over BSE was, arguably, a further example of the precautionary principle in practice – albeit a case where action was forced on a reluctant government by a concerned public. At first the government claimed, implausibly, that it could guarantee that there was no link between BSE and CJD. It then accepted that such an assurance was not possible. But there was still, at the time this change of line was announced, no proof that there was a link; indeed scientists have had some difficulty explaining how one disease could cause the other. The evidence was strong but circumstantial. Nevertheless it was regarded as conclusive enough for the public to take action by avoiding beef, and for other EU governments to ban beef imports from Britain (again overlooking the possibility of baser motives than concern for public health). The burden of proof is with the producer: the farmers will have to prove that beef is safe before people will eat it again.

The Panglossian principle

It is quite possible – indeed likely – that the above analysis is too gloomy about the prospects for the British beef industry. Newspapers will find another story, the fuss will die down and con-sumers will gradually drift back to the meat counters. In which case they will be being guided not by the precautionary principle but by what might be called the *Panglossian principle*. Unless it can be categorically demonstrated that something is wrong, we will assume that all is well. (And, it will be remembered, Dr Pangloss maintained his optimism in the face of some fairly convincing evidence to the contrary.)

Under the Panglossian principle, the burden of proof is with those trying to prove that there is a risk. This is the guiding principle of most environmental policy, from global warming to dog faeces. It is encapsulated most clearly, perhaps, in the report of an official enquiry into leukaemia clusters around Sellafield, the Black Report, published in 1984. A TV documentary had alleged that the incidence of childhood leukaemia in Seascale, the village nearest the nuclear complex, was ten times the national average. There is a well-established causal link between exposure to radiation and leukaemia. The Black Report confirmed the higher incidence of leukaemia, but stated that the link with radiation from Sellafield was 'unproven'. It did not say that it was proven that there was no link. And it offered only 'qualified reassurance' to Seascale residents, hardly very encouraging – carrying even less conviction than the government's current pronouncements on BSE. Yet, since 1984, the government has not only allowed Sellafield to continue discharging the same amount of radiation, it has actually increased the discharge limits substantially. It is as if, in a few years, the government were to relax its rules on the sale of beef offal for human consumption because a link with CJD was still not proven.

A further example of the Panglossian principle at work was the government's approach to the pesticide 2,4,5-T. Agricultural workers suspected that using it was damaging their health, and made representations through their trade union to get it banned. The government agreed to review the evidence – but meanwhile the pesticide would remain in use. The government's advisers then rejected the evidence as merely anecdotal, and stated that 2,4,5-T offered 'no hazard to users, to the general public, to domestic animals, to wildlife or to the environment generally, provided that the product is used as directed'.[11] Of course, the problem was precisely that conditions out in the field often made it impossible to use the pesticide exactly as directed (as they would have done with the animal growth hormones); this was a central part of the workers' case. But the government accepted the advice of its experts nevertheless.

This case appears unsatisfactory not only because the burden of proof was on the victim rather than the producer, but also because of the nature of the proof demanded. This was, as one of the trade unionists subsequently argued, akin to that in a criminal trial: they needed to establish beyond all reasonable doubt that 2,4,5-T was harmful. This they could not do. What they sought to do instead was to show that on the balance of probabilities it was harmful – the concept used in civil law. But this was deemed inadequate by the experts and the government. Exactly the same attitude is being taken today on the issue of asthma and air pollution. One in seven children now has asthma. Urban and rural areas alike suffer from air pollution from road transport. Air pollution is known to exacerbate asthma and bring on attacks. Many doctors and scientists believe that it also causes previously healthy people to develop the disease. The balance of probabilities certainly points that way. But because it cannot yet be proven beyond reasonable doubt, governments are reluctant to act. There is no sign of the precautionary principle here.

Biotechnology: a calculated risk

Biotechnology is hailed as one of the industries of the future. It is high-tech, high profit and high profile. We now have genetically engineered tomato ketchup on our supermarket shelves.

There are super-salmon in the Scottish lochs. And scorpion genes have been released into the Oxfordshire countryside. The bio-technological revolution is underway: the scientists are excited, governments are encouraging, the public, by and large, are kept in ignorance.

The potential benefits of genetic engineering are substantial. The Royal Commission on Environmental Pollution argued in 1989 that:

> Genetic engineering offers the prospect of major improvements in medicine, in industry and in agricultural quality and efficiency. It is also likely to help in dealing with problems of environmental pollution and to lead to new commercial products. The UK is well fitted scientifically to make advances in genetic engineering.[12]

Specific benefits could include drought resistant maize crop for Africa, which would help avert famine and, in the longer term, global food shortages (world stocks are now down to just forty-eight days – the comfortable level is around a hundred days). Genetic engineering may also make it possible to use animal organs in transplant operations.

But there is, of course, a downside. The risks associated with biotechnology are unquantifiable. Adverse effects could be wide-spread and difficult to reverse:

> Organisms which survive and become established could affect the environment in a variety of ways – both beneficial and undesirable. Some releases may alter the diversity of species in the environment, including changing the composition of existing communities. Such effects could produce noticeable changes in the countryside, locally or more widely, and could also have an economic impact, for example if the new organisms proved to be successful predators, competitors, parasites or pathogens of crop plants. Some organisms could pose a threat to human health. At the most extreme, new organisms could conceivably affect major environmental processes such as weather patterns, the nitrogen cycle or other regenerative soil processes.[13]

Or, as two academic commentators put it:

> Perhaps the one thing of which we can be certain is that there will be surprises for us when micro-organisms are released into the

environment ... With scientific optimism, one permits the experiment unless it can be shown to be dangerous; with ecological prudence, one prohibits it unless it can be shown to be safe.[14]

The manufacturers of genetically modified tomatoes, Calgene, have already had one unwelcome surprise. In the summer of 1996 the British authorities gave permission for these tomatoes to be sold in British shops. But until they are grown in Britain none will actually be sold – contrary to earlier plans by the company – because it has been discovered that the tomatoes are far more fragile than normal ones, and have to be treated more like peaches during transportation. This makes the economics of importing them to Britain unattractive.

Since we cannot predict what the effects of genetic engineering will be, the precautionary principle suggests that we should not proceed. This is a point which has been made by Greenpeace and others. Scientific and commercial interests are in favour of taking the risks to secure the benefits: many though not all environmentalists are against. The public, as noted, are generally not involved.

Faced with this balance of competing interests, governments decide, wholly predictably, to go with science and industry. But are they necessarily wrong to do so? The Panglossian principle may be wrong, but does this mean that the precautionary principle is always right? The potential benefits of biotechnology are great, though they may prove unattainable. Are we so risk-averse that we would rather abandon the search than take some chances? Can the risks be reduced or managed to make the exercise acceptable?

Risk management

Where the precautionary principle is not followed, the policy-maker can regulate in an attempt to reduce risk, although as the Royal Society report on risk points out, 'the belief that regulation or other actions can exclude all risk, leaving pure benefit, is a delusion.'[15] In the UK, polluting processes are required to keep toxic discharges 'as low as reasonably practicable' (ALARP) and to use the 'best available technique not entailing excessive cost' (BATNEEC). As these terms suggest, environmental regulation is closely tied to financial considerations – indeed the Environment Agency which came into being in April 1996 was explicitly charged with balancing costs and benefits in all of its activities, despite the difficulties inherent in measuring environmental costs.

As well as emphasizing cost effectiveness, the Conservative government of 1992–7 repeatedly expressed its determination that environmental regulation will be based on 'sound science'. This sounds uncontroversial – who would want it to be based on 'unsound science'? But in fact it is problematic. Science is not wholly objective or free of bias. In the US, it is common to hear people asking the question 'whose science?' A research report funded by an oil company is more likely to throw doubt on environmental claims than one funded by the Sierra Club, a conservation organization in the US. The situation in the UK is not so acute, but it is worsening. The government encouraged scientists to become involved with industry through initiatives such as the Technology Foresight Programme; it is a trend which could be beneficial in helping the UK exploit more of its own inventions, but which reduces the availability of genuinely impartial advice.

This is a problem not just for the public and for environmental groups, but for governments and industry too. Where experts cannot agree, which should be believed? The government stands accused, over BSE, of having listened to those telling it what it wanted to hear – that eating beef was safe. But on what basis was it supposed to make the decision between those experts saying that it was safe and those saying that it was not? Government ministers are rarely scientists, and it would not help much if they were. The Secretary of State would be just one more expert to add to the mix – no more likely, and given his or her other duties probably much less likely, to get the answer right.

Procrastination

It is to get around this problem that governments set up committees of experts. These can be packed with those known to favour a certain viewpoint – this was the charge in the case of BSE. But they need not be. And the greater the number of experts involved, the less likely this will be. Examples of attempts to secure some sort of scientific consensus on which policy can be based include the World Health Organisation (WHO) guidelines on air pollution and the reports of the Intergovernmental Panel on Climate Change (IPCC). In both cases, hundreds of scientists from across the world were involved. Both have led to clear outcomes and recommendations. Unfortunately, both have been ignored in key respects. Even where scientists agree on the main thrust of an issue, there will always be areas of uncertainty, questions requiring more research and consideration. This is where the demand for 'sound science' becomes the excuse for procrastination. Often research becomes an easy alternative to action. I will take two examples.

Lead pollution

The Conservative government refused to recognize any link between airborne lead pollution and child intelligence, despite clear evidence from the US of such a link. It insisted on research being done specifically into the effect on British children, even though there is no significant physiological difference between children in the UK and children in the US. It went on to insist on extra research into the health impact of benzene. Benzene is a known carcinogen, for which the WHO committee said there was no safe limit of exposure – adverse health impacts were possible with even the smallest dose. Petrol companies add extra benzene to unleaded petrol to make 'superunleaded'. The House of Commons Select Committee on the Environment called for the banning of superunleaded petrol, but the government refused (though it did increase the duty to match that on leaded petrol). While it agonized over what to do about beef, which its expert advisers were unsure about, it refused to act on benzene, which experts had confirmed to be lethal.

Global warming

The greatest example of procrastination, however, is the international community's approach to global warming. Real or alleged scientific uncertainty is used as an excuse for pusillanimous inertia. Under pressure from powerful industrial lobbies, even cost-effective, no-regrets policies are ignored. The precautionary principle is comprehensively ignored.

There is, in fact, a remarkable degree of consensus about global warming. No one doubts that a 'greenhouse effect' exists, trapping some of the heat from the sun in the Earth's atmosphere. Without it, life would be impossible. No one doubts either that atmospheric concentrations of carbon dioxide and many other greenhouse gases have increased dramatically since the pre-industrial age, and are continuing to rise. The question is whether increased concentrations of these gases will enhance the 'greenhouse effect', leading to climate change. This possibility has been under consideration by scientists for a century: it was first identified in 1896 by the Swedish chemist Arrhenius. It is thus neither new nor a fad. But given the magnitude of the challenge, governments felt it prudent to try to clarify the scientific thinking. They therefore created the Intergovernmental Panel on Climate Change. This produced its first report in 1990. It produced a second report in 1992. And yet another in 1995. The last of these involved the work of 899 leading international scientists, and confirmed the central findings of the earlier reports. There can be few topics which have been scrutinized so thoroughly, and on which such a broad consensus can be forged. Yet still governments plead 'uncertainty' as an excuse to postpone decisions. Of course it is still possible to find a small number of scientists who deny that climate change will happen, just as it is possible to find doctors who deny the link between HIV and AIDS. Fortunately public health programmes to prevent the spread of HIV were not delayed until this small band of irreconcilables was convinced. Yet this is precisely what is happening over global warming.

Governments are able to get away with this by confusing, deliberately or otherwise, the fact of global warming with the effects it will have. While the former is established, and indeed underway (as the IPCC confirmed in its 1995 report), the exact impacts remain uncertain. This is hardly surprising given the time-scales involved and the complexity of the mechanisms. The impact will be different in different parts of the world. Feedback mechanisms such as cloud formation or local pollution levels will alter the overall pattern. Some generalizations can be made: average global temperatures will increase by between 1.5 degrees and 3.5 degrees centigrade (the last Ice Age was only 5 degrees centigrade colder than today); sea levels will rise; the effects will be greater nearer the poles and less in the tropics; there will be an increase in extreme weather conditions and 'natural' disasters. But the exact impacts will not be known until they occur.

If the effects are uncertain, would it perhaps be prudent to wait until they are clearer before taking action? It would not, for several reasons. First, and beyond the scope of this paper, the policies which are needed – energy efficiency, rational transport policies, reforestation – would be sensible even without the 'greenhouse effect', and many of them would even be good for the economy. Secondly, the effects may not manifest themselves in convenient, gradual and manageable ways, leaving us time to adjust. Third, the global warming that has already occurred is exacerbating other environmental threats which we face. The 1996 ozone hole over the Northern Hemisphere was the deepest ever – levels over the UK in February 1996 were only just over half what they should be. This was the third winter out of four in which a deep Arctic hole has formed. This was unexpected – scientists had predicted that Arctic ozone holes would be uncommon. The reason why their prediction proved inaccurate was that the stratosphere was colder than normal, thus facilitating ozone destruction, because more heat is being trapped in the troposphere by global warming.

Global warming is also implicated in the dramatic increase in what we used to term 'natural' disasters or 'acts of God'. The damage wrought by storms, floods, hurricanes and so on is spiralling upwards. In the first three years of the 1990s, there were twice as many major windstorms worldwide as in the whole of the 1980s, causing damage worth $20 billion. This is why the global insurance industry, the expert in risk assessment, is taking global warming so seriously, why the major companies all have global warming units, and why the insurers lined up with the environmentalists in pushing for greater action at the latest session of international negotiations on the Climate Change Convention. A publication entitled 'Global Warming: Element of Risk' published in 1995 by Swiss Re, a Swiss reinsurance company, sums up the concern:

This hazard has to be contained rather than intensified. And the damage which can no longer be prevented should at least be limited. We have to rethink, correct our mistakes and win time. Instead, public discussion still centres on whether the problem exists at all. And if it does, whether there is any need to react. The answer given by climatologists leaves no doubt whatsoever. We do indeed have a problem, and it is far more serious than would appear at first glance.

The final reason why delay would be foolish is that whatever surprises global warming has in store for us, it is most unlikely that many of them will be pleasant, and the more that can be avoided the better. A 1992 report by the Public Health Laboratory on the potential effect of global warming on health, which the then government chose not to publish, gives a flavour. Among the possible changes it identifies are the reestablishment of malaria in the UK, the reintroduction of permanent endemic plague foci among rural rat populations, the arrival of the heart-worm to Britain, and an explosion in cockroach numbers.

The global gamble

Are decision-makers really concerned about the lack of certainty concerning the exact impact of climate change in fifty or a hundred years' time? It is hard to believe that they are. An instructive parallel can be drawn with economic policy. We have no idea what the economy will be like in fifty years' time, and it would be very hard to get any group of economists to agree on this. Does this mean that we feel unable to implement any economic policies until more research is done?

In fact what decision-makers are doing is grasping at the straw of uncertainty because it enables them to do nothing and hope that everything will be all right after all. In terms of scenario planning, what they are doing is banking on the rosiest scenario – the one which says that the 90 per cent plus of climatic scientists who support significant reductions in carbon dioxide emissions are being unduly alarmist – being the one that comes true. It is as if our defence planners, instead of guarding against the worst case scenario, drew up their strategy on the assumption that no one was going to attack us and peace was assured – a cross between Neville Chamberlain and Dr Pangloss.

But the complacency of decision-makers is not shared by the public. Numerous opinion polls have recorded a high level of concern over a range of environmental issues. One of the most comprehensive, the British Social Attitudes annual survey, found in 1991 that 98 per cent thought that industrial waste in the rivers and seas had a very serious or quite serious effect on the environment, 92 per cent thought the same of tropical deforestation, 91 per cent of industrial air pollution, 87 per cent of acid rain, 85 per cent of nuclear waste and 78 per cent of traffic pollution.

Environmental risks are not perceived to be remote or impersonal. The survey shows that 54 per cent think that the environment affects their health a great deal or a fair amount. People also think that the risks are getting worse: 82 per cent think that it will affect the health of their children and grandchildren a great deal or a fair amount. And people do not trust any political party on the environment. Asked which party came closest to their own views on the environment, 16 per cent said Labour, 15 per cent Conservative and 12 per cent Liberal Democrat; 32 per cent answered 'don't know', and 7 per cent 'none'.[16]

Environmental risk is widely perceived, and politicians are seen to be failing in their response. This contributes to the undermining of respect for politics, the questioning of authority and established practices which is likely to be the pre-eminent feature of politics of the early twenty-first century. Politicians fear the environmental agenda because they believe – in many respects wrongly – that it requires sacrifice and self-restraint from materialist, acquisitive voters. But in ignoring it they not only allow environmental degradation to continue unchecked; they also allow their own profession, and by extension the ethos of liberal capitalist democracy which they seek to preserve, to fall further into disrepute.

Notes

1 C. Tickell, 'Cities and Global Warming', in T. Wakeford and M. Walters (eds), *Science for the Earth* (Wiley, 1995).

2 F. Capra, *The Turning Point* (Fontana Flamingo, 1983).
3 T. Adorno and M. Horkheimer, *Dialectic of Enlightenment* (Allen Lane, 1973).
4 A. Dobson, 'Critical Theory and the Environment', in A. Dobson and P. Lucardie (eds), *The Politics of Nature: Explorations in Green Political Theory* (Routledge, 1993).
5 V. Shiva, *Staying Alive* (Zed Books, 1988).
6 A. Jordan and T. O'Riordan, 'The Precautionary Principle in UK Environmental Law and Policy', in T. Gray (ed.), *UK Environmental Policy in the 1990s* (Macmillan, 1995).
7 Department of the Environment, *This Common Inheritance*, White Paper on Environmental Policy (HMSO, 1990).
8 Royal Society, *Risk Analysis: Perception, Management*, Report of a Royal Society Study Group, 1992.
9 House of Lords, *Drinking Water*, Fourth Report of the Select Committee on the European Communities (HMSO, 1996).
10 B. Wynne, 'Frameworks of Rationality in Risk Management', in J. Brown (ed.), *Environmental Threats* (Bellhaven Press, 1989).
11 Ibid.
12 Royal Commission on Environmental Pollution, *The Release of Genetically Engineered Organisms into the Environment*, Thirteenth Report (HMSO, 1989).
13 Ibid.
14 J. Ravetz and J. Brown, 'Biotechnology: Anticipatory Risk Management', in Brown, *Environmental Threats*.
15 Royal Society, *Risk Analysis*.
16 *British Social Attitudes*, Ninth Report (Dartmouth, 1993).

8

Once the Men in White Coats Held the Promise of a Better Future...

JOHN DURANT

Pity the poor scientists who are deliberating over what should be done about BSE. 'I almost want to crawl into a hole,' one was reported to say. 'I look at the paper and think, my God, we've killed off a £500m export industry. You can't imagine what it's like. But we have to make these decisions and we will.'

Well, I'm not so sure. I'm not so sure that it ought to be scientists alone who make these decisions; and I'm not so sure, either, that in the end the biggest victim of mad-cow disease will be the British beef industry or (heaven forbid) the meat-eating public, but rather science itself. Few debates in recent years have exposed scientific expertise to the harsh light of public scrutiny quite as BSE has done, and given the way the debate seems to be going there is a possibility that the result could be extremely damaging.

It is only relatively recently that science has earned for itself a position of respect in the public domain. A little over a century ago, leading scientists like Thomas Huxley and John Tyndall fought for favour with a British establishment that was more inclined to look to clergymen than to chemists or cosmologists for 'expert' judgements on the issues of the day. By 1900, science had won the ideological battle for cultural recognition; but real political influence didn't come until the experience of world war finally convinced the UK that knowledge was a crucial ingredient in industrial and military success.

Those born after the end of the Second World War grew up in a climate of extraordinary optimism about science and technology. The period from 1945 to 1965 was the heyday of deference to the scientific expert. He (it was almost always he) was the architect of astonishing new discoveries – jet-powered aircraft, atomic power, antibiotics – which were bound to make the world a better place. Hoping to cash in on science's extraordinary success, others aped its methods in supposedly scientific studies of everything from parenting (remember all those postwar childcare 'experts'?) to international politics (much of the mathematical game theory came out of Cold War strategic studies).

This was the time when science was generally regarded as the consumer's friend. In the early days of commercial advertising on television, white-coated experts happily endorsed the latest kitchen gadgets, washing powders, toothpaste and patent medicines. In the high street, the endorsement of the laboratory scientist was an apparently automatic seal of approval, a guarantee that products were not merely new but somehow improved. If science said something was good for us, then it *was* good for us.

Since 1965, several things have conspired to undermine this modernist deference to science. For one thing, the instrumental success of science – itself a crucial ingredient in the rise of the scientific expert – backfired on the reputation of science, as first the disarmament movement rejected nuclear weapons and then the student movement resisted the military uses of science and technology in Vietnam.

Added to this was the growing awareness of the downside of civil research and development in the early environmental movement's protest against pesticides and pollution. In the 1950s, civil nuclear power had been a symbol of scientific and technological progress; by the 1970s, it was widely opposed by people who saw it as a symbol of all that was wrong with so-called advanced industrial society.

Today there is a general sense that we are in transition from modernism to something not so easily described but none the less radically different. Terms such as 'post-industrialism' and 'post-modernism' refer in part to a less monolithic, more pluralist culture in which all the old certainties – religious, political and scientific – are in question. Postmodern culture is altogether less deferential towards experts of all kinds; bishops scarcely count any more; politicians are widely vilified; and even scientists (the latest and in many ways still the most widely respected authority figures in our culture) have a tougher time maintaining their public reputations. In what Ulrich Beck calls the risk society, science is no longer simply regarded as a source of solutions; it is increasingly seen as part of the problem.

The new, more sceptical attitude to science is all around us. It is apparent, for example, in the increasing confidence with which pressure groups such as Friends of the Earth and Greenpeace contest scientific evidence on environmental issues; and it is equally evident in the increasing assertiveness of the consumer movement. Even in the courtroom, traditionally a place where scientific experts were deferred to by judges and juries alike, they have had an increasingly rough ride. In the most widely publicized trial of modern times, an American jury recently turned its back on the bulk of the forensic evidence it had been offered by electing to acquit O. J. Simpson.

This, then, is the context in which British scientists gave advice on what to do about BSE. Two generations ago, it might conceivably have been possible to regard BSE as a reasonably straightforward matter. A new disease of cattle having been diagnosed, the possible risks to other cattle and to humans would have been assessed by a panel of expert advisers and appropriate action would have been put in hand by government. This, in fact, might pass as a reasonable summary of the policy of the Conservative government. The trouble is, though, that we are living in the 1990s not the 1950s: a purely technocratic approach such as this is no longer credible. Listening to government pronouncements about BSE was like living in a time warp; it was as if thirty years of questioning and criticism had simply not taken place.

What is wrong with simple deference to scientific experts on BSE? First and foremost, by their own admission the scientists don't actually know very much about BSE. In fact, their ignorance of the disease – of its origins, of the nature of the infectious agent, or its mode(s) of transmission, or its host range, or its relationship with Creutzfeldt-Jacob Disease in humans – is so great that it is far from clear what solid scientific basis there can possibly have been for many of the confident and frequently unqualified pronouncements about BSE that were issued by the Ministry of Agriculture over the last few years of the Conservative government.

A second problem with deferring to the scientific experts in cases such as these is the problematic nature of risk assessment. In Beck's risk society, risk assessment becomes something of a cult. Today, an almost magical aura surrounds the estimation of probable harm – despite the fact that for the most part such estimation is a mixture of science and speculation. For example, just consider for a moment what is really involved in estimating the risk to humans from the infected brains and nervous tissues of cows suffering from BSE. At one end of a spectrum of scientificity we have measurement of the levels of infectivity in different tissues, and at the other we have the daily business of the slaughtering and dismemberment of cattle. What is the scientific discipline which delivers safe verdicts concerning the reliable separation of risky from non-risky parts of cows?

Even supposing that BSE itself was better understood and that all the relevant risks were reliably calculable, it is far from clear that science alone would provide a sufficient basis for public policy. Public policy must take account of many things: the nature of BSE; the extent of the probable risks; the nature and condition of the beef industry; the state of public attitudes and public opinion; and much else besides. At best, the scientific advisers who have been in the spotlight over BSE for almost a decade are competent to judge only some of these things. Yet at times the Conservative government appeared to lean on these advisers so heavily that the proper boundary between scientific and political judgement was blurred. I should like to have answers to the following questions:

- How, in a situation of enormous scientific ignorance and uncertainty, have scientists allowed their names and reputations to become firmly attached to unequivocal pronouncements by government and industry representatives on the safety of eating British beef?

- Why, in a situation where science, industry and public health are all necessarily involved, have scientists alone been deemed uniquely competent to pick their way through the issues?
- Why, when public confidence was always to be at least as important as public understanding and information, have scientists been left to deliberate the issues in private, without the benefit even of 'public interest' representatives on their expert committees?

Increasing public awareness of the true extent and limitations of scientific ignorance and uncertainty is part of our 'postmodern' condition; it is part of Beck's risk society. Ideally the policy-making process should respond to this awareness by acknowledging the existence of ignorance and uncertainty, and drawing experts, policy-makers and the public into a mature debate of the issues.

In the case of BSE, this signally failed to happen. Instead, we witnessed the old and dismally familiar pattern of bland political reassurance coupled with steadily declining public confidence.

In the present situation, with a major industry under threat and the extent of any public health problem still far from clear, it may seem perverse and self-seeking to worry about the fate of science. But science is important. For all its imperfections, scientific knowledge is an enormously valuable asset. In order to take advantage of this asset, however, we depend on public confidence in science and scientists as credible sources of ideas and information in their appropriate areas of expertise. It would be a tragedy if the misuse of scientific expertise were to undermine public confidence. That way lies know-nothing fundamentalism and, ultimately, the return to barbarism.

Paradoxically, the salvation of scientific expertise in the public domain lies in a greater recognition of the proper limits of science. Our public and political cultures need a greater appreciation of what science can and cannot be called upon to do. Such an appreciation will come in part from a certain amount of well-judged modesty on the part of scientists and, in part, from an opening up of the processes by which scientists deliberate and decide on issues such as BSE. The days are gone when scientists could expect different rules to apply to them: if they wish their views to command public confidence and public respect, then (like everyone else) they must conduct their business openly and transparently.

Without a proper appreciation of the nature and limits of scientific expertise, the public are likely to remain caught between undue deference and undue scepticism about science. As things are at present, we seem to be moving with alarming rapidity from one to the other.

9

There's Method in the Magic

PAT KANE

Defend the Enlightenment! Across the pages and the airwaves, the seminar rooms and the conference halls of the West, this impassioned cry is being raised. According to some of today's greatest intellects – from Francis Crick to Carl Sagan, Noam Chomsky to Richard Dawkins – we are in danger of slipping into a 'New Dark Ages', in which scientific reason is derided and magic thinking reigns. The threat? All the mysticism and super-naturalism that currently grips Western popular culture: whether the prevalence of astrology, the use of alternative medicines, the belief in ghosts and alien visitations, or the search for proof of parapsychology and ESP.

The transatlantic success of the *X-Files*, and the slew of prime-time paranormal shows on British television prove that super-natural belief is, at the very least, a viable market sector – as do the vast expanses of 'Mind, Body and Spirit' shelves in every high-street bookshop, and the huge expansion of alternative health therapies in both public and private realms. According to Paul Kurtz, head of the Committee for the Scientific Investigation of Claims of the Paranormal (CSICOP), this commercial mysticism is pandering to our 'transcendental temptation' – the failing hope that our problems can be solved by an appeal to something beyond rational argument and accepted scientific method.

Yet it is about time we properly engaged with the widespread scepticism about folks who choose alternative medicine, or dabble with non-occidental world-views, or even dream of contact with extraterrestrials (a dream shared by professional astronomers as well as astral channellers and, considering recent news of life on Mars, ever more likely). But what lies at the root of the mass endorsement of mysticism and occult practices is a profound lay mistrust of the authority and consequences of technoscience. The challenge is to find new ways to rebuild a popular belief in science and its applications rather than simply roar out its authority from the laboratory roof.

A restoration of faith in scientific rationality is possible – but only if the scientific establishment is prepared to concede that unreason might well have its reasons. Science must admit its catastrophes as well as its triumphs: it must plumb the darkness that shadows Enlightenment reason. Science must also concede that ambiguity and mystery – for which popular mysticism is roundly decried – is often to be found at the very core of its frontier disciplines. And, finally, science will have to accept that it is always shaped by culture and society – from its theorems to its funding programmes – and that a radically different society and culture may demand a radically different scientific practice.

As we close this century who could deny that the moral balance sheet of scientific achievement is too close to call either way? All the discoveries that underpin the sophistication of the modern world – whether in biology and chemistry, or nuclear physics and bio-engineering, or computation and communication – also serve to subvert that very sophistication.

Bio-engineering makes our food cheap and plentiful, but increasingly disordered and diseased. The digital powers unleashed by the silicon chip replace human labour, mental and manual, rendering many lives socially redundant. Our sense of economic catastrophe waxes and wanes, but the connection between the consumer splendour of the First World, the material despoliation of the Third, and the pollution that smears all corners of the globe is obvious enough without too much prompting from green activists.

All this has recently been gathered under the concept of risk society: insecurity is inevitable in the modern world, in which everyone simply has to rely on rational systems over which they have no control – science being just one of these systems. Our angst about this state of affairs is often traduced as neo-Luddite, a failure to enter into the chance-taking, transformative spirit of the age. Yet have we so quickly forgotten about the biggest technoscientific risk we moderns ever took with our societies: a geopolitical order based on the possibility of global destruction?

After science's vigorous participation in the atomic nihilism of the Cold War – despite the calls for non-involvement in nuclear weapons research from Albert Einstein and Leo Szilard, among others – its claims to be merely a value-free 'servant of knowledge' rang deafeningly hollow. Science facilitated a risk with our very global existence: on the pure level of species survival our mistrust of the Enlightenment's greatest tool is deeply rooted.

In this perspective, science's blithe assertions of pre-eminence among human knowledges almost seem a form of denial. It is as if the scientific community still refuses to face its role in potential apocalypse, refuses to ask what dark motives helped forge these annihilating swords of rationality. Science warriors such as the astronomer Carl Sagan may well characterize popular mysticism as conjuring up a 'demon haunted world', but no demon haunted our world more terrifyingly than Einstein's monster: rationality eager to devour its reasoners.

Yet Einstein's reconceptualizing of matter as a form of energy – the key to unlocking the atom's destructive power – also provides one possible exculpation for scientific rationalism: the strange implications of quantum physics. Beginning with Werner Heisenberg and Niels Bohr, and continuing with David Bohm and Fritjof Capra, physicists have been driven to spiritual speculation by the paradoxical behaviour of the sub-atomic world.

When the same electron can change from a wave to a particle, depending on the position of the observer, what does that say for the classical ideal of scientific objectivity? When particles are split in two, separated by great distances, yet weirdly move in tandem when either one is moved – described by physicists as 'non-local phenomena' – what does that say for the rules of cause and effect? Is there, as David Bohm says, an 'implicate order' to matter that is beyond our present comprehension and presumes a 'wholeness' to all things? Can we conceive of a 'tao of physics', as Fritjof Capra's million-selling book terms it, in which Eastern philosophies parallel the mind-wrenching paradoxes of the quantum world?

Twentieth-century physics has allowed a germ of mysticism into the very heart of science: in the physicist Richard Feynman's words, 'nobody understands quantum mechanics.' The Newtonian conception of science – nature as a machine of parts, comprehensible in its dismantling – has been profoundly shaken. Yet those science warriors who should be the loudest in defence of 'the scientific method' rarely mention such challenges to a mechanistic view of nature.

On closer inspection, most of the scientists who ally themselves with CSICOP's New Age witch-hunts are on the reductionist and mechanistic wing of their own fields. And never mind Mystic Meg: accusations of anti-scientific behaviour are levelled even at their own colleagues. Richard Dawkins, appointed to a chair in 'the public understanding of science' at Oxford and one of the most vocal militant rationalists, takes a highly contentious position in current biology: Dawkins's theory of genetic determinism – the idea that evolution is mainly a vicious battle for survival among 'selfish genes' – is in the forefront of the 'neo-Darwinist' school of evolutionary biology.

This school has vigorous and respectable opponents, who contend that the new Darwinism is overly determined by Calvinist metaphors of struggle, competition and achievement. Brian Goodwin, Professor of Biology at the Open University, accuses neo-Darwinists of ignoring how natural diversity can also emerge from cooperation and complexity, as well as through competition and the 'survival of the fittest gene'. From the University of Massachusetts, the biologist Lynn Margulis has made the remarkable discovery of how the eukaryotic cell – the ancient building block of biological life – was formed from a mutual fusion between prokaryotic cells; again, this proves that cooperation, as readily as competition, can create new and diverse forms in nature.

This is 'good' science, producing 'hard' results; yet what throws down the greatest challenge to our crypto-rationalists are the cultural implications both Goodwin and Margulis draw from their findings. Goodwin is led to argue for a complex 'science of qualities', over a mechanistic 'science of quantities'. As his book

How the Leopard Changed his Spots relates, the struggle of nature – whether the organism be microbe, amphibian or human – is the struggle to express our inner form, our inner structural being, in a creative way. In nature we are all 'emergent forms' together.

Goodwin's science compels upon him a 'holistic view of biological systems', a position which has drawn the charge of 'extreme' and 'mystic' from high-profile science defenders such as Dawkins, and the geneticist Steve Jones.

Margulis's findings pose an even greater threat to the scientific determinists. Her work with James Lovelock supports his Gaia thesis: that an integrated planetary ecosystem, physiological rather than biological, seems to exist. 'Gaia is a tough bitch,' says Margulis, who also attracts much head-shaking in the science establishment over the ideological conclusions she draws from her work.

As for biology, so for brain science. CSICOP's prominent mind–body experts are all classic determinists when it comes to the question of the human consciousness: they include the Nobel Prize winning Francis Crick, the artificial intelligence guru Marvin Minsky and the philosopher Daniel Dennett. Yet consciousness studies, like the biological sciences, is an area riven with debate: those scientists whose work challenges the mechanistic confidence of this rationalist elect are dubbed 'mystic' as readily as any gypsy seer on a lottery show.

Roger Penrose, Rouse Ball Professor of Mathematics at Cambridge, has been caricatured as a 'New Mysterion' for hypothesizing that quantum gravity may have a part to play in the puzzle of self-consciousness. Others, such as the biologist Francisco Varela and the mathematician Ilya Prigogine, compare their computerized models of the 'emergent self' to Buddhist and Eastern philosophies. Their departure from the joyless Calvinist theology implicitly held by the Enlightenment warriors results in a predictable tarring with the brush of mysticism.

From this counter-list of paragons something becomes clear: a new scientific paradigm is emerging. Perhaps it emerges from the shadow of Cold War big science; perhaps it is profoundly conditioned by the gathering ecological crisis. Combining the work of biologists, mathematicians, systems theorists, physicists, this paradigm is what the technology critic Andrew Ross has dubbed 'a kinder, gentler science'. Its vision is one of natural complexity – whether in ecosystems, or societies, or individuals – emerging spontaneously from the space between deterministic order and random chaos: providing what the Santa Fe Institute's Stuart Kauffman, one of its formulators, calls 'order for free'.

This clearly has its resonance with New Age and green dreams of an essentially benign, creative universe. And it may be one possible exorcism of the ghosts and phantoms, angels and aliens that haunt Western popular culture. The new paradigm might not fully return our souls to us from mechanistic science, but it does imply a dynamic, reciprocal relationship between humans and the world they inhabit, rather than the dominant–subordinate one that results in so much technopathology. Perhaps if our explanations of material nature make us feel more at home there, we will not be so tempted to the transcendence of an ideal spiritual world.

Yet we do not need to wait for the next scientific revolution to find practical technologies that begin to blur those firm distinctions between science and pseudo-science. Arthur C. Clarke, the science-fiction writer, once famously remarked that certain technologies, progressed to a certain point, 'would come to seem like magic'. And certain scientific advances are beginning to simulate phenomena that would previously have been consigned to the realm of the paranormal.

For example, we understand telepathy to be the apparently ludicrous notion that one mind could instantaneously communicate with another – without the aid of speech, movement or any other physical medium. Yet Michael Deering, a researcher in virtual reality at Sun Microsystems in California, has pioneered a system by which computer chips are grafted on to human neurons. Ultimately, this will enable thought to be transmitted as microwave signals, as in a mobile phone: another suitably 'hot wired' human could pick these signals up, possibly thousands of miles away. Would this not, in effect, be a form of telepathy?

Another 'thought-controlled interface' was unveiled in London recently, which works by detecting the electromagnetic brain patterns of its users; thus pure thought will fly planes, work computers, guide wheelchairs. Again, is this cybernetic wizardry so different from the ESP notion of telekinesis – the mind able to move external objects by its own internal processes? If there is any frontier of technological advance that begins to collapse those sanctified realms of subjective and objective, it is the human–machine interface. Yet it is a frontier whose horizons look, at the moment, almost infinite.

In short, there is a common culture of intelligent wonderment waiting to be formed, bridging the extremes between scientific fundamentalists and mystical believers, the rational and the holistic. It has begun already in several places. The massive global reach of science-fiction culture – in movies, television, publishing – is premised on an audience eager to speculate about the consequences of present and future science. Physicists now talk seriously about time warps, wormholes through space, and faster-than-light travel; Stephen Hawking has even written the introduction to a new book called the *Physics of Star Trek*.

One notes that Captain Jean-Luc Picard and his matter-transported crew get a very easy ride from the science elect, compared to the channellers and yogic flyers of popular mysticism. SF culture indulges in the same leaps of speculation and the same vocabulary of expedient forces as New Age mysticism, yet science is soaked into its wildest dreams. The defenders of the laboratory may well privately appreciate how much they need space opera to keep scientific method alive.

Star Wars is a more effective defender of the Enlightenment than a thousand hectoring scientists. Perhaps we need some neologisms to describe this culture of possibility – where machines make magic and spirituality computable; where Luddite fears and Promethean hopes beat in the same hearts (and across the same television schedules); where the gulf between the humanities and the sciences is filled with a crackling, unpredictable interaction. Not the two cultures, but a third culture; not supernatural – but future-natural. Maybe not a New Age, or even a New Enlightenment, but certainly a better and more productive argument to have than this phoney war between reason and unreason.

10

Technology and Democracy

PATRICIA HEWITT

This chapter focuses on one aspect of technology – information and communications technology and, above all, the convergence between them. Although the hype around the information super-highway is tedious and often misleading, the comparison with the invention of the printing press is apt: we should recall the rather brief struggle of the Catholic Church to sustain its monopoly over religious truth, and the longer struggle of nation-states to sustain their control over political expression. Like the printing press, the Internet and other powerful networks are inherently democratic: they permit the instantaneous communication of voice, images, text and data between unlimited numbers of people, with no requirement even to know with whom you are communicating. As a result, networks are transforming business organizations and driving companies to flatten the old command-and-control hierarchies. Within business, networks could enable workers, trade unionists, contractors, suppliers, retailers, consumers and share-holders to discover each other, to communicate, and to act in ways over which the company with which these communities are associated will have little control. Within the new political movements, the Internet enables direct action groups to form and re-form with a speed that the organizations they are targeting can rarely match. Networked communities may be vicious as well as virtuous: but for good or ill, networks have started to transform our world.

The impact of convergence arises firstly from the exponential increase in the power of both computing and communication. Gordon Moore, one of the founders of Intel, observed some time ago that processor speed doubles every twelve to eighteen months. Band width tracks microprocessor speed and as speed and capacity go up, prices come down. The prime example, and certainly the fastest growing of the new networks, is obviously the Internet, which most people use through an e-mail application, a facility that anyone working in academia or a reasonably up-to-date business is beginning to take for granted. 'Intranets' – networks specific to an organization – are also growing very quickly, particularly within business. Whether working at home, in the office, or anywhere else, as long as there is access to a telephone socket, employees can connect to a worldwide network, enabling the organization to create and share knowledge capital through what is effectively a virtual library-cum-meeting room of interconnected databases, discussion groups, community pages and so on.

While it is very easy to get carried away by the power and the capacity of the technology, the real significance is social rather than technological. Convergence enables us to transform the economic, social and political environments in which we operate. It enables us to eliminate constraints of time and space and form from everyday life and, in turn, facilitates the creation of new communities which are not bound by geography.

Let me give a few examples of what I think are, in the broadest sense, the political implications of these technology-enabled networks. First of all, this kind of convergence is hugely *destabilizing*. It is the extraordinary power of computing and communications that has enabled the creation of global capital markets which now trade something over a trillion dollars a day. Politically and economically, global capital markets have largely destroyed the ability of national governments to control national economies and thereby to transmit any sense to us that the national economy operates within the control of our own elected government. These networks, and the convergence that underlies them, are also the major drivers of the transformation of business structures and organizations that we see going on all around us, and to which Ray Pahl refers in his chapter.

The second consequence is that organizations no longer need, and most of them no longer have, command and control hierarchies where information is painstakingly passed up to management, analysed and transmitted back down again. To give a very mundane example, every time you go into a supermarket, the checkout operator (particularly if you have a loyalty card), simply by scanning your purchases, is now also fulfilling the function of the market researcher and stock controller, although without being paid for both those other jobs as well. Organizational structures and job design are constantly changing in a process whose most visible, certainly most politically visible, manifestation in industrial societies is that middle and senior managers are losing their jobs. However much economists may argue that there is really not any great difference either in the numbers of jobs or in how long people remain in employment compared with the 1950s, the fact remains that what people thought of as lifelong jobs – the jobs in IBM, for example, or the Civil Service or banks – are no longer there. The result is real insecurity, and an even greater *perception* of insecurity, among a class of men who had previously felt some control and predictability in their lives.

Technological change can be both empowering and disempowering for different groups of people. Breathless discussion of 'knowledge workers' is beginning to give way to a more detailed understanding of how networks enable control of front-line and lower-level workers to be embedded in the work design itself – a post-industrial equivalent of Taylorist control over the speed of a factory conveyor belt. In quite a large number of jobs in the modern economy – including data processing clerks, telephone sales operators, customer service centre staff – the speed of output, the number of keystrokes per minute or telephone calls per hour, the quantity and the quality of sales per hour can all be instantaneously recorded and analysed within the software application staff are working with. Crucially, the results can immediately be fed back, not merely to their supervisor, but to the workers themselves and to their peer group, so that work control is embedded in the technology that is enabling the work performance. An interesting field of study is just beginning to open up in assessing the sociological consequences for people working in this kind of environment.

We see other forms of transformation. Coming back to what I said earlier about removing constraints of time and space, we see how more and more work can be done remotely. Work teams across the globe can share information and knowledge, make decisions, design and test entire products, without necessarily having to meet face to face or even work at the same time or in the same time zone. Indeed, one of the latest Boeing engines was designed, tested and flown, in a virtual sense, by precisely that kind of virtual global work team. The face-to-face service of the kind people used to get and still occasionally get in a bank branch, for instance, is increasingly being replaced by an interactive kiosk or, at a much lower level of technology, simply a telephone service like First Direct. This person-to-person communication is supported by people working in a remote call centre which does not even have to be in the same country as the person whose bank account they are facilitating, let alone in the same immediate community.

More often we read, particularly in management literature, about the empowering effects of the new technology. It is argued that as you spread information downwards and outwards, you make possible much greater knowledge, creativity and responsibility among front-line and lower-level workers. This can be seen happening, too, although knowledge workers in this sense make up fewer numbers than some authors would like to believe.

We need to draw attention to an emerging paradox within modern business organizations. On the one hand, as Ray Pahl rightly observes, the constant change which is now an organizational cliché produces a disruption of traditional localities and sources of security. In striking contrast, however, is the emphasis in leading-edge management thinking and best practice on just the reverse – the need for loyalty and commitment, for responsible and creative relationships within the business organization and indeed within its entire supply chain. Technology may and does enable the construction of those relationships across the world, but without an effective understanding of how *people* create and maintain relationships, the potential of the technology is unfulfilled. Throughout the literature on learning organizations, for example, we find a constant theme about how organizations can facilitate risk-taking and the making of mistakes without which there is no creation of new knowledge. There is ample survey evidence from this country and elsewhere that the essential quality that employers now look for in a new employee is the ability to work as part of a team. Computer literacy can be acquired, but emotional literacy (to use Susie Orbach's term) is the real prerequisite for effective relationships in the workplace – for making networks truly successful.

Returning to the IT-enabled networks themselves, we should note the impact of convergence right across the supply chain of businesses. We are all aware of the growing intensity of competition as organizations increasingly source their operations from almost anywhere in the world. Once again, the immediate effects for those working in higher-cost locations are disempowering, a loss of security. There is, however, the potential in global supply chains for quite different effects, if suppliers start to make common cause or to form direct links with the customer. Consumer and user groups are already active on the Internet, swapping information about price, quality and complaints for a particular manufacturer's products. In the field of health care, there is an explosion of patient and self-help groups of both the physical and the virtual kind. With the sharing of medical information on a growing number of specific diseases, patients and families begin to know far more about their condition than almost any family doctor they are likely to consult. In the political arena, direct action is now facilitated by convergence, with animal rights and environmental groups using the Internet to keep well ahead of the authorities. That in turn suggests the scope that exists for consumers, shareholders, pension fund contributors, trade unionists and a wide variety of other groups to make common cause by sharing information and knowledge.

There is an interesting question here about what convergence means for conventional politics and for relations between citizens and government. Although a few Members of Parliament and government departments have put home pages on the Internet, and the political parties use e-mail for routine communication in election campaigns, these are very small uses of the power of the network that is available. We have yet to see an established political party use those networks to transform their political culture: not to feed information and instructions from top to bottom, but to create a much more open-ended and fluid form of dialogue and participation.

Finally, I want to end with a reflection on the issue that is so often raised in discussion of information superhighways – the fear that economic division will be mirrored by a division between the information haves and the information have-nots. We need to avoid falling into the trap of assuming that the information haves and have-nots will necessarily be the same as the economic haves and have-nots or the employment haves and have-nots. I am not sure that we know at the moment who is most at risk of becoming an information have-not. To take one example: Andersen Consulting and Nationwide have developed a virtual building society branch in the form of an interactive multimedia kiosk that has been extensively tested in live trials. Most of the young men and women who built it assumed that older customers would be put off by the technology and would head for the comfort and safety of the real person behind the desk. Quite the reverse. In fact, elderly customers are taking to these interactive kiosks with enormous delight. One of the unexpected reasons for this is that they would much rather ask a machine what they fear might be a stupid question than ask a real person, particularly when they are holding up a queue of people behind them. So we cannot assume that information haves and have-nots will map on to the demographic map that we are familiar with and used to dealing with.

We know also that some of the undereducated young men who are most vulnerable to the transformation taking place in the global economy are often brilliant when it comes to video and computer games. In that context, one of the most interesting projects I have seen was when I was deputy chair of the Commission on Social Justice, on a visit to a project in Belfast which had been established and inspired by an equivalent project in Harlem, New York. In Harlem it is called 'From Bullets to Bytes', in Belfast it is called 'Bytes for Belfast'. In Belfast, they have created a series of community centres, or additional rooms in community centres, equipped with state-of-the-art technology. They have staffed it with young men and women and have simply thrown it open to teenagers. Overtly, the intention of the project is to show these youngsters that the skills they take for granted, the skills they regard as 'playing', if you like, in the computer arcades, are actually the skills of which an economic future can be made. But at the same time the primary purpose of the project is to enhance the self-esteem of these often very disadvantaged, alienated, disconnected young people by giving them something that to them, and indeed to us, is highly valuable. This is the kind of project that we might want to look at as part of a broader policy programme which uses technology to transform public places in order not only to make the technology universally accessible but, in the course of doing so, perhaps changing relationships between individuals as well.

I began by drawing an analogy between the convergence of information and communications technology, and the invention of the printing press. In both cases the technology is not really the point. Technology can be enabling and sometimes disabling, but ultimately what it enables and what it disables is up to us. Which brings us back to the central issue addressed in this volume, to politics and power.

11

People in Distress

SUSIE ORBACH

Every day of the working week, I sit in my consulting room listening to people in distress. At the centre of their concerns is a wish to be living their lives unencumbered by the chronic anxieties, the insecurities, the despair, rages or depressions that cloud their daily lives. Although the recent media coverage of psychotherapy, psychoanalysis and counselling might incline one to think otherwise, therapy is not a soft option, a kind of massage of the soul, a self-indulgent fifty minutes, or a faddish part of the lives of the well-heeled and well educated. Rather psychotherapy is invariably a treatment of desperation, sought when other means for transformation have been exhausted: when friends, families, lovers, teachers have failed to provide a context, a way of seeing, a relationship in which the pain that so troubles the person can be addressed.

At the heart of the analysand's quest and at the core of much despair is the struggle for a reliable self, capable of speaking about the texture of their experience and being understood and accepted by others. There is great longing to break out of what can be felt as a trap in order to achieve what is felt to be missing – contact, emotional exchange, the giving and receiving of love, satisfaction from one's work and the chance to express oneself as part of the human community, in which one's uniqueness, one's sense of authorship of one's own life is enhanced.

Psychoanalysis's field of study is the human subject. Psycho-analysis theorizes about the predicaments at the heart of the human condition. In seeking to explain and relieve impediments to living, it traces the intra-psychic mechanisms that are available when psychologically indigestible experiences occur. It maps the internal world of the individual and the way in which external experience is incorporated. Like poets and artists, psychoanalysis ponders what makes for an enlivened existence. What makes life an endurable, even a pleasurable adventure?

In being given the brief to talk about how to build quality relationships, there is an implicit notion that psychoanalysis can be prescriptive, that there is a formula for building good relation-ships, a preferred developmental pathway, a set of policies that psychoanalysis can offer to society.

While I don't think psychoanalysis can do that, because as a discipline it is essentially not prescriptive, it nevertheless *has* learnt a tremendous amount during the last hundred years about human relationships. Although this knowledge doesn't immediately trans-late into a set of policies, the study of the individual subject in distress has a lot to contribute to a revitalized modernist project; to the understanding of what human beings require; to the emo-tional conditions that make it possible for human beings to thrive; and to the environmental provisions that make engagement with the world an enlivening and enjoyable activity, rather than an enervating, draining or threatening experience.

Of late, we are used to family relationships being used for pol-itical gain by politicians who, misunderstanding either wilfully, mendaciously or ignorantly the complex texture of emotional life, make a rhetorical call for a return to family values, to the two-parent idyll that never was – the presumed idyll from within which most of my patients and the patients of my colleagues were raised. The family is re-visioned as a harmonious supportive unit in which conflict is managed, responsibility taken on readily and in which parents parent. Economic pressures, shifts in gender relations, the collapse of the health and education services, wor-ries about work, about the ubiquitous penetration of consumer culture into the core of all of our identities, the hurts of racism and class are all miraculously meant to be absorbed and pro-cessed in the family. The family is seen as both bulwark against

society and a treatment plant for society's sewage. The tensions
between parents and children, between the sexes, the demands on
women to care for the elderly and the young, the restructuring
of work in which fewer jobs are stable, the crisis of masculinity,
in other words, the very things that make individuals and groups
of individuals unstable, are – instead of being engaged with in the
political debate – given a sleight of hand or, worse, even a dose
of ideology to cover them up: 'not us,' say the politicians, 'it's the
destruction of family values that is to blame.'

Now, of course, there is a part of what our political leaders are
talking about in their nostalgic call to the family of the immediate
postwar period that speaks to us. And as it speaks to us, it acts
as a temporary balm, because the search for certainty, for stability, for security is something we can all relate to. We crave these
in the face of political, economic and social uncertainty and we
crave these in the face of lives lived with insufficient emotional
sustenance.

But let's be clear what sense we can make of our desires today.
The image of the family unit is the gossamer over which we
stretch our needs for attachment, for intimacy and autonomy:
needs which seem central to the way humanity has developed in
the West. Where our politicians and policy-makers are inclined to
look at the forms of attachment, we do well to look rather at the
content of attachments. Where we fantasize stable, guaranteed
relationships, hearts and flowers romances, we do well to look
rather at what intimate human engagement requires and supplies,
what makes relationships work. Most importantly we need to
recognize that one of our human dilemmas is that relationships
can be especially adhesive when they are patently destructive.

Part of what psychoanalysis allows us to see is that when the
early environment can provide relationships in which the developing child can have its initiatives responded to with care, when
the needs of the child can be held in mind and thought about
in ways which convey to the child the essential okayness, the
legitimacy of its desires – that is to say its very essence – the child
grows up with the emotional base to be a partner in creating
and maintaining attachments which are secure and stable. It can
manage, inside of itself, the consequences of disappointment, of
things going wrong.

The original relationships which surround a developing child can be thought of as the food for emotional growth. If the food is reasonably nutritious, the child will thrive. It will have absorbed the flow between itself and others as benevolent and it will have internalized a self-regard which allows it to engage with its wider environment with a confidence about its capacity to manage its needs, its interests and the disappointment of them.

In our earliest relationships, we absorb a mass of information about the world we are born into. Depending on our particular circumstances we take in the sense of whether differences between people can be managed, whether emotional responses can be textured and complex or are required to be monochrome, about inequalities and differences. We also learn something about our own impact, our agency. We sense what it is about us that can bring pleasure, can evoke responses in others. We don't process these phenomena at a conscious level, but the prolonged period of language and motor development, the fact that human beings only develop recognizably into what we call human within the context of relationships, indicates the crucial nature of early life.

Where early life fails to give the individual the recognition and relating that it requires, in relationships where needs go not so much unmet as unrecognized, the individual's development is marked by inner conflict. She or he will experience a lack of self-regard along a continuum from insecurity to self-hate. The hurtful relationships cannot be left, or given up for more satisfactory ones. The unsatisfactory relationships are manacles which may bind the person, not only to the original relationships, but to the shape and emotional pith of that original relationship for ever more. To put it starkly: if *satisfactory* relationships in early life incline one to seek out their repetition, so does the influence of *unsatisfactory* relationships. We are disposed to repeat what is, even if that has been felt to be insufficient, for that is how inside of ourselves we experience relationships. We know no other.

Where early relationships have been problematic, several processes are set in train. There is an invisible withdrawal from the world of actual relationships – that's to say, people look as though they are relating quite ordinarily, they have lovers, they play, they work, they procreate, etc. – but a part of them is split off and preoccupied with internal relationships. In these internal relationships, which analysts like to call object relationships – both to distinguish them from actual relationships and to demonstrate that they are relational scenarios which are available for psychic manipulation inside our heads – the person repositions herself or himself, not so much as a passive victim of their circumstances, but as a central actor in his or her emotional drama. They hurt, they don't receive the love, they can't activate their energy and so on because they haven't yet located the key that would render their love object, and what they still require from them, more available to them. In this process, it is not so much that they are powerless as uninspired. They haven't yet come up with what it is they need to do to instigate what they want from the other.

One aspect of this preoccupation with internal relationships can be a process of searching to please the other and, by so doing, restoring it to value, so that it can in turn be giving. This, however, involves a further adhesion to problematic relationship configuration. The extent to which the object has failed the person is in direct proportion to the level of its idealization. The greater the disappointment, the more unsatisfactory the relationship, the more, in the unconscious, is that person wanted. Meanwhile, in the outside world, the experience of disregard or of unsatisfactory relating will predispose the person to unwittingly seek, attract and confirm that experience in new relationships, even as they try to challenge it. The channels for receiving that which doesn't meet the expectations, are closed.

Internalized bad relationships can't then easily be given up. They are hard to digest and be done with. They linger and fester, unleashing emotional havoc on others, binding up psychic energy, so that engagement in the world is often reactive rather than creative.

Now I say all this to stress that what we require in trying to build quality relationships in a risk society is that we focus on enabling relationships and the enabling aspects of relationships rather than the specific form of relationships. In this way we might contribute to and shape that society rather than feel ourselves to be constantly reactive, blown off course and rushing to catch up with it. While it can be argued that the manic defences which arise out of disabling relationships also allow for a certain kind of lively embrace and interpretation of the new, they can also bring with them an adaptability which is addicted to change and sensation rather than to engagement with the substance of real experience.

What we require as individuals, as groups of individuals, as a society, are relationships which provide us with an emotional security. Emotional security is the basis of autonomy. Particularly in times of rapid, unmapped change, the capacity to embrace what is and to think and to act out of that thoughtfulness to tolerate the insecurity inherent in many aspects of our lives, depends upon the internalization of enabling attachments.

One thing that skews our relationships is our gender arrangements and especially the disposition of emotional dependency needs between men and women. For years women and men lived with the myth that women were dependent and men independent. But the emotional dependency needs of men and women can be more brightly illuminated by turning this equation upside down and asking the question: on what is men's independence based? What underpins and supports men's apparent autonomy? What makes it possible for men to feel able to take on challenges in the world, in so far as they have; to take a personal authority, to feel unburdened by deep insecurities? What emotional services have men historically received that have sustained their sense of independence? What twist has allowed women to be conceptualized as emotionally dependent when it is obvious that their role has been to provide a relationship on which others may depend without anticipating such a relationship for themselves?

I am not arguing that men are dependent and women are not. I am suggesting that in any consideration of how we build quality relationships, and the means to adapt to the challenges of risk society, the question of the disposition of emotional dependency needs and emotional capacities between women and men needs to be confronted and the issues of autonomy and dependency, and their relationship to one another, understood.

Emotional dependency and autonomy are central to an understanding of human resilience, creativity and agency. Autonomy grows out of a sense of emotional relatedness; it is a consequence of a reasonable attachment. I want to stress this because I think we have unexamined attitudes towards the notion of the individual, of autonomy, of dependence, of independence and that these unquestioned and unreflected positions bolster a set of defences which need deconstructing.

We need not remain mystified about what makes enabling relationships. Relationships that enable are those which allow for a full experience of the other, and for a range of emotional responses to be registered rather than interfered with. They don't consist of carving up emotions and letting men carry one set and women another. Adults who can ask of one another how they are and stick around for a genuine reply without trying to fix, transform, deny, or ridicule the responses they get are providing enabling relationships. Quality or enabling relating depends on a certain level of emotional literacy; the capacity to resonate with another emotionally without being swamped, to empathize without feeling impelled to make better, to register one's personal emotional responses in all their subtlety, so that there is space for those responses so often disregarded because they are undramatic. Enabling relationships depend upon an equal emotional exchange and a certain emotional fluency. Enabling relationships sustain us in the ambivalence of our responses. They make it possible for us to hold contradictory feelings simultaneously rather than retreat into emotional fundamentalism where all is good or bad or love and hate and where scapegoating – projecting – dominates our relation to self and others.

This is what I mean when I say we do well to address the content rather than the form of relationships. Because if we can begin to take what psychoanalysis has learnt about human psychological development, about what makes for the embrace of the world and what makes for the destructive acting out on it, what makes for the emotional capacities we require – the routes of which I have only been able to hint at here rather than elucidate – we can offer a kind of thinking to policy-makers that reaches the parts that social reform, guided only by economic, social and political considerations, fails to get to. We can enhance policy by understanding what it is that provokes our individual and social responses both at a private and a public level. (I'm thinking here of a suggestion by Andrew Samuels for the psychotherapist to be included along with the statistician and the economist on government committees.)[1]

In a discussion about what individuals require in this changing economic and social milieu, there must be a consideration of an individual's capacity for adaptability, for invention, for taking up the challenge and the conditions that make that likely. We need to understand the experiences of childhood that can contribute to that and the structures for adult life that can then fulfil the needs of children and grown-ups. A focus on the content, the texture, the quality and basis of the commitment of relationships is the valid place to start. Rhetoric which addresses form is a non-starter.

The political agendas from feminism, from educators, from mental health and the new parenting organizations as well as those that focus on emotional literacy link up here, in ways that coincide and perhaps surprise our current policy-makers who would set these constituencies in opposition to one another.

For twenty-five years, feminists have been pushing for child care and parental leave arrangements that can engage all those who parent rather than mothers exclusively. They have also argued for the active participation of men in the rearing of children. These calls have attracted educators and parenting organizations, who have seen the results of the absence of men in parenting as well as the impediments to the active and engaged parenting which men may desire.

There is also a challenge to the way work is organized and a call for its redistribution so that we no longer support a division between the overemployed and the underemployed. Such policies are supported by parenting organizations and even progressive corporations, who for different reasons want to provide the economic and social supports to those who parent in whatever family arrangement, so that the emotional quality of those relationships is strengthened.

The policies sound straightforward enough, and indeed some policy-makers have gone some way along the road to thinking through their implementation. This needs to be supported. Clearly we need policies which have as their focus, not ways to shore up or return to a traditional family structure, but policies which free those parenting to learn to relate to children in the steady, dependable ways that all human infants need in order to become autonomous effective adults. We need policies that encourage emotional literacy for those who are already adults. The task is far from easy. But we do know that concentrating on the form of relationship rather than the content sows a field of dragon's teeth which sprout into the manifold difficulties with living and working that we so often see today in our consulting rooms.

The capacity to manage complex emotional lives is a political issue. It makes for a robust population who can think about the wider political issues rather than being emotionally manipulated by them. Who can refuse the false conflation of the private and the public and who can open up new issues in the public agenda.

Note

1 As discussed at Antidote, an organization which promotes emotional literacy.

12

Friendship: the Social Glue of Contemporary Society?

RAY PAHL

It is a truth universally acknowledged that when challenged on what should be their central concern, most politicians will echo Bill Clinton and reply, 'the economy, stupid'. Yet as the 1990s draws to a close, there is a growing awareness that 'going for growth' with 'the enterprise culture' is not necessarily producing a more contented and happier society. Poverty confronts us in the streets, surveys report people's fears about crime and disorder, and moral entrepreneurs claim to detect a failure in the quality of family life – 'the parenting deficit', in Etzioni's phrase.[1] So, if the politicians in the 1980s called on economists to justify their rhetoric, the pendulum seems to have swung back in the 1990s and they begin to look to those who are specialists in understanding society – rather than simply the economy – to justify a new rhetoric.

Since politicians have neglected to pay the same attention to sociology as they have paid to economics, the language they use to describe our social ills is often imprecise and confused. There is talk of fragmented societies and the lack of social cohesion, coupled with a somewhat frantic search for some effective social glue that will, by implication, recreate or reconstruct a 'better' society, such as was perceived to exist in some previous golden age. In the past it may be assumed there was a political divide between those who sought to conserve the putative social qualities of a previous age and those who sought to create a better future order, whether based on gradualist evolutionary change or something more cataclysmic. Those of the latter persuasion were devoted to a vision of socialism as the 'active utopia', in Bauman's phrase.[2]

Such a political divide no longer exists and politicians at all points in the spectrum are left in a muddle. Those who look to a 'strengthening of the family', for example, can be found as much on the far left as the far right, if, indeed, these words continue to have any significant meaning. Other panaceas that have been invoked include citizenship, communitarianism and social-ism.[3] These tended to flutter brightly in the media for a while but did not appear to stand up to careful scrutiny. Those who advocated active citizens did not expect to be confronted with images of silver-haired granny figures in front of bulldozers on the line of the Newbury bypass, or appearing at the dockside with sticky plaster over their mouths bearing strongly dismissive epithets, as they attempted to prevent the export of calves. Communitarians were, perhaps, harder to dismiss, since it was very difficult to see precisely what was being proposed. If the parenting deficit was seen to be both true and unacceptable, then, presumably, parents would have to spend more time at home or, alternatively, widespread, affordable childcare and nursery provision would have to be provided. If the former, then enthusiastic communitarians would have to be very careful not to give the impression that they wanted women to disengage from the labour market, so that they would be free to welcome their children back from school with home-baked teas. If the latter, then the cost would deter all but the most committed advocates. Similarly, if communitarianism implied a nostalgic adoption of village-like 'communities', then there was no way of imposing such a vision on an admittedly fragmented and divided society. Previous mechanisms of creating social solidarity, such as geographical isolation or common involvement in a particular locality-based occupation, such as mining or shipbuilding, no longer apply, as they have long been destroyed, apart from some idiosyncratic exceptions.[4]

Finally, the social-ism that has been mentioned by Mr Blair appears little more than a rhetorical alternative to a now discredited individualism. When unemployed people were urged in the 1980s 'to get on their bikes' in search of employment elsewhere, it was not intended that such a philosophy would apply to men and women who were emotionally less attached to their partners. Commodification of labour power is one thing: commodification of quasi-sacred family relations is quite another. It is hard to expect men and women to make moral commitments to each other as partners when such moral commitment is encouraged to collapse between employer and employees and, possibly, between a welfare state and its citizens, although, as subjects, British people should not perhaps have very high expectations. The rejection of selfish individualism is understandable, but is the appropriate response an espousal of social-ism?

The collapse of the socialist project in the late 1980s and the ill-considered quick-fix panaceas that have briefly flared up to replace it in the years that followed have produced a vacuum for political rhetoric about the nature of the good society. Furthermore, certain fundamental issues have fallen out of political debate. However, it can be shown that industrial societies with a more egalitarian distribution of wealth and income are healthier, have less crime and their inhabitants are generally happier. Sadly, however, this will not necessarily lead to a potent political debate on the social advantages of greater equality. The search, therefore, is for social glue in an increasingly inegalitarian society. It is important to bear in mind that the search for a society 'more at ease' with itself, in John Major's phrase, cannot be divorced from the way the reward structure of society is determined by the political process. Sociologists are obliged to address the problem of social cohesion in Great Britain in the late 1990s, recognizing that this is being done in a context where the processes leading towards greater inequality are not being seriously restrained by government policy. We start therefore with a considerable handicap.

For the rest of this essay I hope to eschew the political rhetoric and to focus on the actual pattern of social relationships with which people are involved. My argument, in broad outline, is that there appears to be a long-term secular trend towards more individual choice, not simply in matters of personal consumption in the market, but also in connection with a wide range of personal relationships. As Giddens and Zeldin show in their distinctive ways, people are engaged in transforming dependent relationships of one sort or another into confluent relationships.[5] Men and women are gradually learning to talk to one another as equals. As people gain in emotional confidence they are learning to escape from fixed roles, whether achieved or ascribed, in order to relate to others as distinctive individuals with true selves. This search for a sense of self, an individuality outside role-given behaviour, is a very powerful force for social change. Women seem to have discovered the need first, as they began to rebel against being 'just a housewife' in the early 1960s. Men clung on to their occupational identities longer, but as both traditional and working-class solidarities and traditional middle-class career stability were undermined one after the other, men's anxieties and insecurities began to increase. The privatization of the career may turn out to be the most radical privatization of them all.

In the same way that men have had to learn not to seek for a female partner as a substitute mother, so they have had to forego the sibling-style support of trade union or professional organization. As institutional supports for identity crumble and partners struggle to learn to negotiate distinctive identities for themselves, without the traditional props of role identities to help them, there are bound to be casualties. Couples split and partners reunite with others in the hope of negotiating better and more rewarding identities for themselves. This has consequences for others, especially their children. More complex patterns of stepfamilies emerge with new roles and new identities which have to be formed or found.

In much public discussion of the family, attention is generally limited to one set of family relations at one stage in the life course, namely parents with school-age children. This may sometimes be extended to include the responsibilities towards elderly parents. There is much less concern with siblings, cousins, aunts, uncles and the whole complexity of stepfamilies. An attempt to measure the frequency of contact between family members suggests that these contacts with all types of relatives have fallen in the last decade.[6] This is probably due to women's increased commitment to the labour market, leaving them less time for visiting parents or their adult children.

Another possibility is that friends are taking over from given families as new 'families of choice'. As the proportion of marriages that end in divorce increases and as men and women move geographically, and perhaps socially, from their family of origin, so friends come to provide continued support and security. Evidence from the British Household Panel Study shows that both men and women who are divorced are more likely to see a close friend during the previous week than those who are married.[7] Furthermore, a recent report in the British Social Attitudes survey, while showing a general decline in the proportion of respondents seeing a relative or a friend at least once a week between 1986 and 1995, found that the decline of those who reported seeing their best friend at least once a week was relatively small – less, for example, than the decline in those who saw their mothers at least once a week. Indeed, respondents in 1995 were more likely to see their 'best friend' during the previous week than any other relative or other family member (not sharing the same household) – some three-fifths of the sample claiming to do so.[8] In earlier research, Peter Willmott has shown that middle-class people relied more on friends for help when a child was ill or for babysitting. For both social classes he showed that friends were more important than relatives or neighbours for providing help with shopping, home maintenance, keeping an eye on the house and providing practical help on a day-to-day basis. Friends were also crucially important as confidants.[9]

Those friends whom people have known since school or college serve as anchor points in their lives and can help to provide emotional integration and stability. Since they know about the other's strengths and weaknesses, triumphs and failures, they can more readily be non-judgemental in the face of their friend's troubles at work or at home. In a seemingly more risky world, where neither employment nor family relationships may be able to provide an enduring sense of security, certain kinds of friendship may provide a vital source of happiness and affirmation of personal identity. Evidence to support such an argument empirically is notoriously difficult to achieve. Unsurprisingly, survey research shows that while money cannot buy happiness, it certainly helps. Leaving that aside, there is a clear positive relationship between having friends and being happy. Analysis of friendship network data from the 1985 NORL General Social Survey in the United States demonstrated that 'especially close' friends provide more positive results for happiness than simply having many friends.[10] Of course, as with many such large-scale social surveys, it is hard to be sure whether people with close friends are made happier or whether happy people are more likely to make close friends. Sociologists have attempted to measure how far the social support provided by a social network of friends and acquaintances leads to better health, greater happiness and longevity of life.[11]

For the purposes of the present discussion, I do not want to be distracted into a detailed discussion of the empirical significance of social networks on individual and social well-being. Rather, I want to focus on the importance of a particular kind of friendship, which I wish to distinguish from other kinds of less intense and more superficial relationships with people who may also be called friends. From Aristotle and Plato to the present day those wishing to understand the personal, social and political importance of friendship have attempted to deconstruct the notion into qualitatively different elements. Following Aristotle, one can distinguish between friendship based respectively on utility, on pleasure and on character.

Much friendship is little more than acquaintanceship: a category of friend that we are happy to compartmentalize in different sections of our lives. A friend with whom we watch football or go to the cinema is not necessarily the one we get to help us to buy a piece of furniture or whom we may meet from time to time for a drink. Such social friends are useful and tend to be the people like ourselves whom we spend time with before settling down with a partner. Later such social friends may help with school rotas and child care. These are useful friends and we generally keep a close watch on the balance of reciprocities in order not to get into a goodwill deficit.

Another type of friendship is based on the attempt to reproduce for adults what an ideal family would be for children. Such friendships provide help, comfort and protection from the impersonal and sometimes harsh and competitive world of employment and market relations. The woman who listens sympathetically when people come to her with their troubles and confusions serves as a supportive mother figure and may enjoy the feeling of having a permanent dependent 'family'. The young professional who adopts a senior colleague as mentor may be enjoying a son-like role he is unable to relinquish as he gets older. People who need these kinds of friends are still trapped in family-like roles and may not yet have the confidence to move beyond them. Some sibling-like relationships are at the boundary of this kind of friendship. Siblings are typically at the boundary of family relationships as they extend social links horizontally, while most family relation-ships are vertical.

The third type of friendship is about knowing and being known. It is about communication. It is liberating and it is fundamentally egalitarian. This is what Aristotle called 'character friendship'. This pure form of friendship is to some extent subversive of social institutions and social roles. Not everyone has either the capacity or the opportunity to enjoy such friendships. Some who are sur-rounded by social, utilitarian and relatively superficial friends of the first sort may be afraid of the openness implicit in this third type. They may prefer to keep each social friend in a separate compartment so that no one can see them 'in the round'. They have not enough confidence or self-esteem to develop a pure friendship. Those in the dependencies of the second type have not yet grown out of wanting to dominate or to be dominated.

In a more open, changing and fragmented society, friendship relations may suffuse family and kinship relationships and, indeed, move beyond them. We keep close contact with those members of our families whom we most enjoy being with – siblings, cousins, in-laws. Our obligations to those whom we also value as friends will be considerably stronger.

People in employment, living with partners also in employment, are frequently under serious time pressure. Friends need time – particularly those pure friendships which are crucial in forming an individual's identity or in helping that person through a crit-ical time of change. It is understandable for this and for other reasons that people should seek to combine their relationship of pure, closest friend with that of sexual partner. This may be convenient but it puts great strain on one particular relationship – expectations may be higher than can be satisfied, given all the other practical pressures involved in domestic divisions of labour.

This raises problems. Friendship does not always settle down easily with family roles. Friendship is exclusive and inclusive. We are not obliged and may not wish to be the friends of the friends of our friends or to know anything about their families. They come as they are. Partners, however, bring parents-in-law, and possibly children from a previous marriage and so on: responsibilities and reciprocities are built into the relationship. Yet, increasingly, people are seeking to escape the sometimes suffocating, if not damaging and emotionally disturbing, aspects of their family of origin. Child sexual abuse and intrafamily violence indicate widespread unsafe havens in a heartless world. Partners, unwittingly or otherwise, force confrontations. The role of grandparents and step-grandparents can be benign and supportive; sibling rivalry may not exist; parents-in-law may delight in the addition of the partner to the family circle. But, sadly, such universal support is not always to be found. The current fashion for books revealing personal accounts of the authors' childhood memories of fathers and mothers illustrates very well the skein of conflicting and semi-repressed experiences and emotions which surround our closest families ties. Many have to leave their family of origin behind them in order to develop their true selves. Adult relationships free from dependency and the emotionally suffocating echoes of family life reflect an individual's growing maturity.[12]

Different forms of love and friendship can, of course, be combined. Partners may come together through the power of romantic love, move into a type of mother–son dependent relationship and later, with age and maturity, move into a communicating friendship. This implies a substantial growth in maturity which not all can be expected to manage.[13]

Friendship, in the terms in which I am addressing it, can be seen to be subversive of established social institutions and social forms. It is inherently anarchistic; it is fundamentally opposed to the market mentality and possessive individualism. Friendships are diminished in moral quality if the terms of the exchange between friends are consciously or scrupulously monitored, for this would imply that utilities derived from friendships are constitutive, as in market relations, rather than valued as expressions of personal intentions and commitments. As Silver, one of the few sociologists to explore the idea, puts it:

> Such friendships are grounded in the uniquely irreplaceable qualities of partners – their 'true' or 'real' selves defined and valued

independently of their place in public systems of power, utility and esteem. Friendships so conceived turn on intimacy, the confident revelation of the self to a trusted other, the sharing of expressive and consummatory activities. Ideally, friends are orientated to the tensions and meanings that give rise to acts, not the publicly stand-ardised meaning or import of acts. The behaviour of friends to each other is appropriately interpreted through knowledge of the other's inner nature, not the content or consequences of actions. The privacy of friendship is not only cultural but formal: no body in law and administrative regulation brings sovereign authority to bear on friendships; while others may pass censure or render judgement, friends have the right and capacity to ignore them.[14]

There is a case, then, for arguing that pure friendship is a reflection of the contemporary concern for individuality (not, let it be noted, individualism, which is associated with the discred-ited project of the neoliberals of the 1980s). Such friendship is voluntary and embodies 'a very positive image of human social relations not realised elsewhere in capitalist society'.[15] Since it involves mutual self-awareness it accommodates itself well to the reflexivity characteristic of late modern society.[16]

Modern friendship cannot be assumed to be the same kind of social relationship as existed in ancient Greece or eighteenth-century England. Arguably, the modern, pure form of com-municative friendship is the most personal relationship possible, expressing an ideal of voluntary personal agency. Only in modern society, argues Silver, has it been possible 'to create a democratised arena of elective affinities, in which persons culturally value each other for their true, that is their unproductive selves'.[17]

Significantly, the kind of friendship to which I am referring is perhaps less likely to exist in the same way among the poor. In Carol Stack's classic study of the support system of black women, many of them lone parents, one of them is quoted as saying:

> Some people don't understand friendship. Friendship means a lot, that is if you can trust a friend. If you have a friend, you should learn to trust them and share everything that you have. When I have a friend and I need something, I don't ask, they just auto-matically tell me that they are going to give it to me. I don't have to ask. And that's the way friends should be, for how long it lasts. But sometimes when you help a person they end up making a fool

out of you. If a friend ain't giving me anything in return for what
I'm giving her, shit, she don't get nothing else. These days you ain't
got nothing to be really giving. You can't care for no-one that don't
give a damn for you.[18]

So, for the poor, friendship has of necessity to have an instrumental aspect to it. The free, expressive and, in principle, unlimited generosity of pure friendship may be a luxury which, while
it can be found among poverty-stricken bohemians or advocates
of alternative or suppressed political movements, is, in general, to
be found among those with some surplus to distribute. However,
someone with too great a surplus in relation to the friend is in
danger of killing the friendship with kindness.

Pure, communicative friendship is based on moral principles
which are in conflict with market exchange as the major principle
for the intellectual ordering of the political world. Some might,
therefore, view friendship as a threat to the smooth and harmonious functioning of the social order, since friends and lovers may
withdraw emotional energy from a wider range of institutional
roles and relationships. Hutter writes:

Friendship and love present the lure of deeply-satisfying relationships
at the expense of the networks of casual involvements, so needed
by society, from which the individual necessarily has to withdraw
some power of feeling for the purpose of investing this power in
love and friendship. All deep loves and friendships thus are akin to
a form of regression from higher levels of social organisation.[19]

Societies respond to this potential threat to social institutions
either by seeing friendships as a private matter for individuals in
which the state takes no interest, or by incorporating friendship,
albeit in a somewhat weaker form, into such areas as conflict
mediation, banking and finance and political control. However,
whether it is perceived as a private or a public matter, friendship
cannot but have political implications.

First, friendship can be dangerous and disruptive. In political
purges of all types, to be a friend of a victim is a highly dangerous position to be in. Stalin's victims were often under horrify-
ing pressure to betray their friends. Family connections could be

readily discovered: true friends were potentially more dangerous but more easily hidden. A traditional Russian fable describes a captive prince's willingness to sacrifice wives, children and retainers, all of whom could be replaced, but when, by chance, the victor slaughters the captive prince's friend the prince then breaks down in misery. Persecutors are quite often right: conspiracies are frequently organized around the ideals of friendship. Partners in crime make strong partners, the status of an outlaw providing a strong impetus for the formation of friendships.

The second political implication of friendship is that it is fundamentally egalitarian, and one of the strongest barriers to pure friendship is structurally conditioned inequality. One good measure of the existence of a class-stratified society is the empirical existence of structural divisions or faults reflecting the normative, relational and economic aspects of class. Friendship links that cross putative class boundaries would serve to undermine arguments based on the immutability of given class structures. Typically, strong pressures exist in class-structured societies to avoid the formation of friendships between unequals. This may, for example, involve the sanctioned rules of exclusion and inclusion, such as those determined by parents for their children or rigidly segregated eating arrangements within institutions and organizations. Rules of social distance are rigidly practised at the top of British monarchical society and there are reflections of this throughout society. A truly friendly society would, of course, be a classless society, and so, logically, giving a greater centrality and salience to pure friendship could be a powerful force for social change.

Finally, it should be recognized that having someone as a friend is a form of power which those without close friends do not have. It takes power to maintain friendships, but communicative friends have it as their goal to move beyond power games to a situation where both voluntarily renounce power. Aristotle's perfect friend is simply an alter ego. With such friendship the Self is known to the Other more completely than in other relationships and this, of course, implies greater vulnerability. Such openness implies trust. Trust, a precondition of friendship, implies the absence of fear and with such trust there is also freedom to be truly one's self and to do what one truly wants to do.

An anxious person is less able to develop this open friendship, since Self, in a state of anxiety, is drawn in on itself in anxious self-examination. In such an anxious state, to quote Hutter again:

> Self presents an inauthentic image of itself to the outside world. Thereby it gains a shadowy confirmation of its own reality through its mask. The more Self, however, lives through its mask, the less it becomes known to another, the more shadowy does its core become. The further this process of bifurcation in Self between inner and outer has gone, the more precarious and difficult does it become for Self to reveal itself in friendship to another. The greater the split, the greater the leap of trust Self would have to make in order to establish the base of openness from which a friendship relationship could develop.[20]

This echoes Aristotle's view that perfect friendship is only possible among people who are good, having overcome their hatred and fear of themselves and each other. Perfect friendship is therefore an ideal which men and women may strive towards but not expect to reach.

The overcoming of the negativity of the Self requires a vision of the good which the Other must share. This need for value concurrence is crucial. Through such a shared vision of the good, friendship becomes a relationship which is essentially creative of the Self.[21] This is why, in an age which is much obsessed with identity, true self and a sense of personal individuality, the development of pure, communicative friendship becomes a more generalized social, as well as personal, goal.

The fact that there are both private and public dimensions to friendship can make friendship dangerous to the wider society. Individuals make their commitment to each other without reference to group-derived status, norms and values and are likely to withhold information about the internal structure of their relationship in terms of its guiding norms and values from the outside world. Seen in these terms, as Hutter put it, 'every friendship is thus a potential culture in miniature and also a potential counter-culture.'[22]

Since one of the fundamental rules of friendship in all cultures is that gifts are given freely without thought of return, then friendship always tends towards equality between people. Friendships between people of widely divergent status, abilities or backgrounds are much less likely.

Friendship is a relationship built upon the whole person and aims at a psychological intimacy, which makes it, in practice, a rare phenomenon in its purity, even though it may be more widely desired. It is a relationship based on freedom and is, at the same time, a guarantor of freedom. A society in which this kind of friendship is growing and flourishing is qualitatively different from a society based on the culturally reinforced norms of kinship and institutional roles and behaviour.

If I am correct in detecting this emerging aspect of contemporary social change, the consequences for our political system could be far-reaching. It could be the basis for a new style of social relationships. It is fundamentally egalitarian, individualistic and exclusive. In a sense it is antipolitical. It is a more mature social form than one based on dependency, superordination and subordination. It is subversive of market-based social relations: pure friendship is based on generalized reciprocity. The introduction of quasi-accounting procedures undermines the very essence of communicative friendship. In contrast to the individualism of competitive market capitalism, where individual failure is an essential ingredient of the effectiveness of the system, individuality is about distinctive style and identity – it is not about hierarchies and effectiveness, but the unique capacity of everyone to be potentially lovable. Admittedly this raises problems for those with difficulties in forming secure adult attachments. It implies that in order for a citizen to be fully engaged in a good society, access to material resources is not enough: access to psychological resources is also necessary.

There was a time when the image of the voter was limited to a person in an institutional or economic role – trade unionist, organization man, bureaucrat, manager of the domestic economy, reproducer of labour power or whatever. Early socialism was based on the sibling-like solidarity of fraternalism and male bonding which moved on to the caring mother model of the postwar welfare state. Conservatives tended more to a paternalist mode – being a more or less kindly father, doing what was necessary for the family business to continue without unnecessary interruption. Voters/children were to be seen and not heard and should be grateful for whatever was done for them and should certainly fight for their rulers when told to do so. Admittedly this shifted to a determination to make the children stand on their own feet and not be 'moaning minnies', in Mrs Thatcher's phrase, always asking for a helping hand instead of just getting on with it. Politicians fall easily into fatherly or motherly roles, chiding voters for not recognizing the difficult time they have in providing for 'the family', that is, all of them, and keeping United Kingdom plc neat and clean and safe.

Rarely do politicians relate to voters in a truly unpatronizing and friendly way, expressing their feelings and hopes as one friend might to another. Nor do politicians let us see them as people enjoying pure friendly relations: we see them formally as mothers and fathers or patrons and clients, yet their close personal friendships remain hidden from view.

If the family is the chief model for political relations, with much parliamentary debate being, as it were, a struggle between the authority of the father and the authority of the mother, this produces a highly directive, secretive and exclusive style of politics. The voters as children or siblings can do little more than react to what is done on their behalf. They cannot engage as friends. The more the political process is centralized, the greater will be this tendency. The principle of subsidiarity, to locate responsibility for decisions and actions at the lowest possible level, is certainly more friendly.

The larger formations of social life – kinship, the law, the economy – must be different where there is, in addition to solidarity and dutiful role performance, a willingness and capacity for friendship's surprising one-to-one relations. This difference alone may be enough to transform social and political life.

It is possible that progress in democracy will depend on a new generation that will increasingly locate itself in identity-shaping, social and yet personally liberating friendships. These sociable individuals who are striving to express themselves completely in friendship are, in a sense, deinstitutionalized. They do not see themselves primarily as housewife, trade unionist or manager. They are women and men who enjoy music, the countryside, the arts and who work to live, not live to work. A voluntary association such as the one for anglers may have more members than does the Labour Party. How people live and who they are will be more determined by their friends than by their mothers or their superior line managers. We find out who we are as people with and through our friends. Friendship is about hope: between friends we talk about our futures, our ideals and larger-than-life meanings. There is an idealism in strong friendship because it is detached from the fixtures of role, status and custom.

A consideration of the politics of friendship is certainly not a new idea. There is a long line of political theory from Aristotle to Hannah Arendt which has focused on friendship. Love, whether romantic or affectionate, is basically unpolitical: as Hannah Arendt writes, 'because of its inherent worldlessness, love can only become false and perverted when it is used for political purposes such as the change or salvation of the world.'[23] Love, then, is a powerful antipolitical force, as its intimacy or closeness results in the destruction of the public space among persons. Friendship, by contrast, plays an important part in Arendt's political theory, since, for her, friendship signifies a companionship with others as equal partners in a community common to them. Friendship in the Aristotelian form of *philia politike*, similar perhaps to respect, has a dimension which is seen by Arendt as 'a regard for the person from the distance which the space of the world puts between us'.[24] This, clearly, is a looser form of friendship than the pure, communicating form I have been emphasizing so far. She is referring to a particular style of relationship based on the recognition of and respect for differences and heterogeneity among friends. Distinctively, Arendt is following the ancient Greeks in recognizing in friendship a unique discursive reality:

> For the Greeks the essence of friendship consisted in discourse. They held that only the constant interchange of talk united citizens in a *polis*. In discourse the political importance of friendship, and humanness peculiar to it, were made manifest. This converse (in contrast to the intimate talk in which the individuals speak about themselves), permeated though it may be by pleasure in the friend's presence, is concerned with the common world, which remains 'inhuman' in a very literal sense unless it is constantly talked about by human beings. We humanise what is going on in the world and in ourselves only by speaking of it and in the course of speaking of it we learn to be human.[25]

This appears to place private conversation and debate at the centre of political life. Friends talk of their shared interests and concerns; disagreement will not necessarily lead to animosity or the break-up of the friendly relations. Arendt appears to equate this kind of continuing talk and discussion among friends as the inner essence of Socrates' distinct mode of politics. Political friendship, thus conceived, has a direct parallel with Aristotle's dictum that 'friendships seem to hold cities together' since it is claimed to have the capacity to mould collective identity or community among peers. It is evident that, for such a model of political life to work, time must be found for the basic discourse or conversation, and it does not, of course, follow that this talk among friends is always about 'getting our message across' in the naive belief of some politicians. It may equally be the basis of politics of resistance or rebellion. This is a point frequently overlooked by communitarians. Arendt sees *amor mundi* as describing 'citizens' dispassionate and yet dedicated commitment to the welfare of the world' which becomes the main 'driving power by which they are propelled to an adventure in the common world'.[26] Shin Chiba concludes an analysis of Arendt's view with the hope that 'this vision of citizens' politics of freedom based on political partnership . . . should serve as an inspiration for political action in the twenty first century'.[27]

It may now be objected that I have done little more than replace the fluffy notion of communitarianism with an apparently equally fluffy notion of friendship. In what way is my friendly society any different from the socialist active utopia or the neoliberal combination of market, family and strong institutions such as the legal system? I suggest that it is between these extremes that many now hope that a basis for a more humane and creative politics may emerge.

A friendly society is built out of real existing relationships and not the wishful thinking of traditional socialists or neoliberals. There can be little doubt that at the end of the twentieth century the forces that have encouraged people to make more choices for themselves, to seek to express their own individuality by the clothes they wear, the houses and consumer goods they buy and countless other ways from body language to their views on opera or rock music, apply also to their choice of social relationship. People are concerned about their identities and seek a way of living in which they can express their individuality, but they are not overwhelmingly secure: they need confirmation of their identities.

Furthermore, they do not want the pattern of their private lives to be imposed on them. They want to become independent of their parents, they want to express their sexual orientation in their own way – the idea of reverting back to arranged marriages as a way of strengthening the family in a form that may exist in other societies today is a ludicrous notion.

So the twentieth century has seen a long march towards a freer, more open style, where people choose their friends and relish their freedom. Partners who try to control the other's friends on grounds other than the potential disruption of the partnership would be held to be unreasonable. People need, seek and, if they are wise, cosset their friends. Parents may die, children leave home, partners may split up, but friends can supply the crucial binding cord of a person's life. Unlike more nebulous concepts such as 'community', it is perfectly possible to investigate an individual's set of social relationships very precisely and the analysis of social networks is open to some mathematical sophistication. This is where the strength of sociology and social anthropology should be revealed. Sociologists have documented patterns of friendship for men and women and related these to a variety of social and institutional variables. Friendship can be very precisely described in its patterning, usefulness and relationship to kinship. All this provides a useful descriptive story.[28] Social anthropologists tend to go further, being much more interested in the political importance of friendship, generally at a local level. Mediterranean anthropology is particularly rich in such analyses. Sadly, few anthropologists have done much work on friendship in non-peasant societies, although there a few notable exceptions.[29]

In this essay I have intentionally avoided summarizing research on the sociology of friendship in contemporary Great Britain, since these studies do not generally pay any attention to the politics of friendship in the Aristotelian sense. There is a curious gulf between the theories of political philosophers and the detailed ethnographies of sociologists and social anthropologists. My position has, in a way, been more polemical. I have argued that as people focus more and more on sustaining and maintaining distinctive identities that are not formally provided by family or employment, so the social meaning of friendship will continue to increase in salience. There is still a long way to go and this is a social trend whose impact may not be felt until well into the next century, but what I am describing is an essential social fact of late modernity. Many people are very sophisticated in assessing the impact of new information technology on our institutions, politics and way of life. The fact that there are also fundamental qualitative changes in the way we relate to each other is not considered with the same attention or sophistication. If, as I argue, people are moving towards an ideal of pure communicative friendship as the kernel of their lives, then this may well have far-reaching implications.

But there is, of course, a fundamental problem with friendship: we cannot call our friend to account if he or she fails us in any way. Of course, friends complain to each other and strive to avoid causing pain or embarrassment. But just as friendship cannot be bought, so it cannot be maintained without trust. Friends do trust one other: they have to. So, in a society in which there is considerable mistrust in most institutional spheres, the growth of friendship is a hopeful sign. Unlike the nostalgic utterances of communitarians, we can confidently assert that most people do have friends and that these friends structure or certainly influence the way we see ourselves and how we see and relate to others. This, I suggest, is likely to have long-term political consequences and may, in part, help to contribute to the collapse of the party system and the dominance of the power of Whitehall. About all this there will surely be much debate and I hope that some of the themes I have opened up in this chapter will help to encourage a more informed discussion on the possibilities and consequences of a friendly society.

Notes

1 A. Etzioni, *The Parenting Deficit* (Demos, London, 1993), an edited and adapted version of *The Spirit of Community* (Crown, New York, 1993).
2 Z. Bauman, *Socialism: the Active Utopia* (Allen & Unwin, London, 1976).
3 On citizenship see the Commission on Citizenship, *Encouraging Citizenship* (HMSO, London, 1990). For a lively collection of essays see G. Andrews (ed.), *Citizenship* (Lawrence & Wishart, London, 1991).

For a brief statement of communitarianism by Amatai Etzioni, addressed to a British audience, see 'Common Values', *New Statesman and Society*, 12 May 1995, p. 245. Tony Blair first refered to 'socialism' in his speech to the Labour Party conference in October 1994.

4 For a more extended discussion of this point see Ray Pahl, 'Friendly Society', in S. Kraemer and J. Roberts (eds), *The Politics of Attachment* (Free Association Books, London, 1996).

5 A. Giddens, *The Transformation of Intimacy* (Polity Press, Cambridge, 1992); T. Zeldin, *An Intimate History of Humanity* (Minerva, London, 1995).

6 See the following table from R. Jowell et al. (eds), *British Social Attitudes: the 13th Report* (Dartmouth, Aldershot, 1996), ch. 3: Francis McGlone, Alison Park and Ceridwen Roberts, 'Relative Values: Kinship and Friendship', p. 58.

Percentage of respondents seeing relative/friend at least once a week

	1986		1995	
	%	*Base*	*%*	*Base*
Mother	59	643	49	1026
Father	51	477	40	822
Sibling	33	1092	29	1702
Adult child	66	420	58	812
Other relative	42	1218	35	1796
'Best friend'	65	1224	59	1768

Bases (numbers of respondents) exclude those without the relative in question, as well as those living with this relative.

7 The following tables from the British Household Panel Study, Wave 4, 1994, show the proportion of those who made contact with a 'close friend' (not spouse or partner) by writing, visiting or telephoning during the previous week.

By age and sex, 1994

	Men		*Women*	
Age	*%*	*No.*	*%*	*No.*
16–29	84	1247	88	1315
30–59	70	2279	82	2510
60+	65	914	75	1216

By marital status, 1994

	Men		Women	
	%	No.	%	No.
Married	68 (76)	2571	80 (85)	2685
Living as a couple	73 (82)	382	83 (90)	391
Widowed	77 (70)	146	77 (82)	605
Divorced	79 (87)	164	89 (89)	301

The percentages in brackets relate to Wave 2, 1992, when the definition of 'close friend' could include spouse. In both waves 'close friend' could refer to a relative.

For further results from the study, contact the ESRC Research Centre on Micro-social Change, University of Essex.

8 See note 6 above.
9 P. Willmott, *Friendship Networks and Social Support* (Policy Studies Institute, London, 1987).
10 Felix Requena, 'Friendship and Subjective Well-Being in Spain: a Cross-National Comparison with the United States', *Social Indicators Research* 35.3 (1995), pp. 271–88: 'In the US it is more important to have better friends than many friends. On the contrary, in Spain people pay more attention to get a high number of friends but intimacy is less important' (p. 281). In Spain family relationships are more important than intimacy. This bears out the suggestion that a shift from family to friends as confidants is part of the trajectory of modernity along which the US has advanced further than Spain.
11 See Michael E. Walker, Stanley Wasserman and Barry Wellman, 'Statistical Models for Social Networks', in S. Wasserman and J. Galaskiewicz (eds), *Advances in Social Network Analysis* (Sage, London, 1994) and the references cited therein.
12 See Giddens, *The Transformation of Intimacy*, and Kraemer and Roberts, *The Politics of Attachment*. A particularly useful approach to different forms of friendship is provided by Graham Little, 'Freud, Friendship and Politics', in R. Porter and S. Tomaselli (eds), *The Dialectics of Friendship* (Routledge, London, 1989).
13 See Susie Orbach's chapter in this volume.
14 Allan Silver, 'Friendship and Trust as Moral Ideals: an Historical Approach', *European Journal of Sociology* 30 (1989), pp. 274–97, at pp. 274–5.
15 P. Abrams and A. McCulloch, *Communes, Sociology and Society* (Cambridge University Press, Cambridge, 1976), p. 44.

16 A. Giddens, *Modernity and Self-Identity* (Polity, Cambridge, 1991).
17 Silver, 'Friendship and Trust', p. 295.
18 C. Stack, *All our Kin: Strategies for Survival in a Black Community* (Harper & Row, New York, 1974), p. 57.
19 H. Hutter, *Politics as Friendship* (Wilfrid Laurier University Press, Waterloo, 1978), p. 6.
20 Ibid., p. 13.
21 I have found much the clearest exposition of this interpretation of Aristotle's views on friendship to be J. M. Cooper, 'Aristotle on Friendship', in A. Rorty (ed.), *Essays on Aristotle's Ethics* (University of California Press, Berkeley, 1980).
22 Hutter, *Politics as Friendship*, p. 19.
23 H. Arendt, *The Human Condition* (University of Chicago Press, Chicago, 1958), pp. 51–2.
24 Ibid., p. 243.
25 Quoted in Shin Chiba, 'Hannah Arendt on Love and the Political: Love, Friendship and Citizenship', *Review of Politics* 57.3 (1995), pp. 505–35, at p. 522.
26 Ibid., p. 535.
27 Ibid.
28 For a useful and very accessible introduction to the sociological literature see G. Allan, *Kinship and Friendship in Britain* (Oxford University Press, Oxford, 1996).
29 There is a very large anthropological literature which it is not appropriate to cite at length here. I am thinking of the work of F. G. Bailey, John Davis, Julian Pitt-Rivers, Eric Wolf and many others. A classic contribution is by Robert Paine, 'In Search of Friendship: an Exploratory Analysis in "Middle-Class" Culture', in *Colloquium on the Comparative Sociology of Friendship* (Memorial University of Newfoundland, 1969), pp. 505–24.

13

The Politics of Prevention

MARTIN WOOLLACOTT

'Never predict anything, particularly the future,' Sam Goldwyn reportedly said. But the prediction of dangers ahead has become such a central activity that it increasingly defines both individual and collective life. Above all, the containment of future dangers has, without our quite noticing it, gradually become the main business of government.

We are the risk society, in the notable phrase of Ulrich Beck, composed of people constantly calibrating risks in our personal lives and with a deeply established expectation that the job of the political class is the avoidance or minimization of future risk for the whole society, and the provision of compensation when this fails.

Whether it is lung cancer or mountain climbing, Chernobyl or the Chunnel, global warming or single parenthood, ecological threat or worrying social trend, the theme is the same: predict, warn, avoid. The dangerous future casts a long shadow, and politicians ignore it at their peril. As Beck writes: 'We no longer tolerate the fairy tale of the unforeseeable consequences. The stork does not bring consequences. They are *made*.'

Whole scientific establishments concern themselves with the prediction of risks. Newspapers and television, on some days, seem concerned with little else. The Green political movement, after many vicissitudes now assuming a pivotal importance in the most powerful European state, has grown out of risk prediction and prevention. The complicated relationship between public perception of future risks, expert assessments and political calculations – demonstrated recently during the Brent Spar affair – seems to many to have become the most vital, and difficult, area in the politics of industrial nations. The huge importance of insurance, the industry which specializes in risk, has come home to us with the troubles at Lloyd's of London and the increasingly panicky discussions about pensions. These raise as an issue not so much the misfortune of investors who took foolish risks themselves, but the fearful possibility of an uninsurable world – a place where no conceivable premiums could cover the likely losses. Here there is a parallel between the commercial insurance that asbestos, hurricanes or negative equity could undermine, and the social insurance that unemployment or increased survival into old age could overturn.

The difficulties of the welfare state are just one category within this panorama. They provide a good example of how the risk prevention style doubles back on itself: first creating a risk prevention structure, and then in turn warning that the structure may fail. As we become more and more adept at the forecasting of at least some risks, we become more and more preoccupied with it, and more and more demanding in our requirement that government take the responsibility for the management of risk, and the provision of compensation when that management fails.

Is this any more than saying that government is about what it has always been about, namely security? It is, because the predictive, highly detailed and comprehensive modern concept of security makes it different from the older tradition of providing defence, law and order, and some broad economic guidance. Is it any more than saying that the rise of the welfare state has induced an expectation of protection among citizens? It is, because the old welfare state was mainly about retrospective help for those who had fallen on hard times. The risk society is about identifying dangers *before* they arrive, including dangers arising from the effects of welfare measures. The political point is that future risk can only be scientifically measured and managed collectively. The provisions government must make are not only to protect citizens against some of the risks they take as individuals, but about managing the whole body of risk.

The risk society's origins lie in the modern revolution in prediction and risk assessment. This flows from many sources – scientific and medical research, actuarial research, more sophisticated insurance, and from futurology, which in turn had its beginnings in the operational research of the Second World War, culminating later in the establishment of the think tanks. From the Rand Corporation on, the study of the military enemy and what he may do next grew into a comprehensive study of all the 'enemies' the race might face in the future, from overpopulation to irradiation, from dictatorship to disease.

The generalized association of government with the avoidance of risk in wealthy societies is so rooted in expectations, so much a part of both right-wing and left-wing political traditions, that it will survive any trimming of the welfare state. And it is likely to mean that politicians who think that they can rid themselves of responsibility for risk by pushing state functions into the private sphere, or creating 'third party' authorities to carry the can, are going to be gravely disappointed. There can be no return to the sort of ignorance about the future that characterized governments in the nineteenth century. 'State shedding', or the process by which a more modest state narrows the range of its activities and lets its citizens take risks 'on their own', could turn out to be the biggest illusion of the turn of the century. However much they twist and turn, politicians cannot escape their role as risk managers.

This is increasingly the case when the future is seen as more and more threatening. Beck has written of the transition from a society where the central political problem is the 'distribution of goods' to one where the central problem is the 'distribution of bads'. Citizens demand that the bad consequences of industrialization and modernization be at best avoided, at second best reduced, and in any case *equalized*, on the principle that they must not be suffered disproportionately by any group or class.

The recent poll indicating that the majority of Britons have 'lost faith' in the future, thinking that it will be worse than the present, is another piece of evidence suggesting that pessimism has become the natural attitude of ordinary people. But there is a contradiction, one of critical importance, in the popular mood. Pessimism does not mean that government is expected to do less, but that it is expected to do more. Pessimism about the future is powerfully allied to the expectation that government will steer through the dangers and that it will provide compensation to individuals who are nevertheless injured – whether they are hoodwinked pyramid scheme investors, asthma sufferers, Gulf War veterans, or survivors of football stadium fires.

The New Right in Britain and America often seems to argue as if the only part of the population 'dependent' on the state's management of risk were single mothers and the unemployed. In truth the entire population, class by class and group by group, is wedded to the idea that they have a right to protection from and compensation for risk. That, in a sense, is what modern government is *for*. There is no escape from the culture of warning and the politics of prediction, prevention and compensation.

14

Risk and Public Policy: Towards a High-Trust Democracy

ANNA COOTE

The 'risk' paradigm suggests that we live in an uncertain world where we cannot control or predict accurately what will happen to us. Yet it also insists that we cannot just throw up our hands and leave everything to the postmodern equivalent of fate. We can try to understand how little we know, and engage actively and positively with our uncertainty. We can take responsibility, individually and collectively, for negotiating and shaping our future. But that requires a more mature relationship between people and politicians.

Candour is to the politician as twelve pints of lager is to the prima ballerina. When Stephen Dorrell, Health Secretary in the Conservative government, made his announcement about the possible dangers of eating British beef, it hit us like a bolt from the blue because it was an isolated moment of candour against a background of sustained, systemic dishonesty and distortion. No wonder he was greeted with howls of derision and outrage. It was a breach of the convention that politicians always have an answer to our questions, that there is always a fairly simple answer, that they always have the right answer and therefore need never change their minds or disagree with their party colleagues. If, in truth, they don't know the answer, they admit it at their peril. They will be skewered by the tabloids, roasted by the *Guardian* and eaten for breakfast by John Humphrys on the *Today* programme on Radio 4.

There is in fact a kind of collusion. The public, the media and the politicians all know, or at least suspect, that there is a huge amount that ministers do not know, or cannot know, but we expect them to bluff convincingly. We need them to be certain, partly because there are so few points of certainty in our lives, and partly because we relish the ritual slaughter when they are found out.

We like to act out the charade of having a child-to-adult relationship with our politicians. We are the children, they are the grown-ups. They are supposed to be able to answer our questions and protect us from the hazards of life. In fact over the last twenty to thirty years we have grown into our teens. We still expect them, on one level, to be infallible. Yet we are learning that they are not and consequently we despise them. For their part, the politicians kowtow to us, like parents to difficult offspring, because they are scared of triggering mood swings, sulks, withdrawal of love and affection. They don't expect a mature response.

The implications of the risk society for the conduct of public policy-making is that we must grow up and develop an adult-to-adult relationship with our politicians, as well as with scientists and all manner of so-called 'experts'.

An adult-to-adult relationship does not imply that everyone knows the same as everyone else, but that we all know something, that no one is omniscient. Ideally we respect each other's knowledge and experience – we are not overawed or diminished by any of it, nor are we slighting or disdainful. We interact and are interdependent, as human beings who are different but equal.

The fact that we are still caught in our early teens in our relationship with politicians may explain why non-politicians who offer themselves for elections do so well. Berlusconi, for example, or Ross Perot. Perhaps Ronald Reagan, the actor turned *ingénu* politician, paved the way. Undoubtedly, Margaret Thatcher's popularity depended on the fact that, in one vital respect, she was not like any other leading politician. We are so thoroughly disgusted with politicians that we are prepared to give our vote to any oddball or fanatic so long as he or she is not a 'normal' politician. But we have to learn the hard way that this new brand of mould-breaker is not necessarily any more trustworthy than the conventional model.

New Labour, of course, is presented as a mould-breaker. The message has been: 'we are new, we are young, we are a breath of fresh air.' It seems to have a strong appeal to the electorate. It implies 'we are not like all the rest, so you can trust us.' This sounds promising and may be true. But it is not the same as striving for an adult-to-adult relationship.

We have heard that the 'culture of contentment' has given way to the 'insecure majority'. The insecure majority requires a high-trust democracy. The mutual respect which is integral to an adult-to-adult relationship implies a degree of trust in the other. Not blind faith. But the kind of measured confidence that comes from informed understanding. Trust has broken down because politics is characterized by secrecy, spin-doctoring and special pleading. We can only rebuild it by moving forwards, not backwards. There are two backward-looking strategies which some have adopted as ways of dealing with the new mood of insecurity.

The first is the authoritarian response, based on pessimism, nostalgia and the desire to reclaim traditional methods of control. Thus policies are produced which seek to prohibit divorce or penalize lone parenthood; which seek to crack down on crime by heavier punishment and more incarceration. Beneath the authoritarian response is a desire to replace politics, which is about negotiating change, with a semblance of morality, which is about conserving absolute values. We need clear values, yes, but these must resonate with the real, changing world in which we really live; they must be understood and shared as widely as possible. Moral values can provide a context for political decision-making, but not a substitute for it. A high-trust democracy is built on understanding and consensus not on instruction and obedience.

The second backward-looking strategy is that in an uncertain world we can simply leave the market to solve our problems. If new risks arise, then the market is bound to produce new strategies for dealing with them. Ever more sophisticated methods of risk assessment, ever more imaginative insurance schemes. This is backward looking in that it repeats the mantra of the eighties, which seemed to many like a good idea at the time, but has thoroughly revealed its limitations.

Undoubtedly, the market will respond to new kinds of risk and provide us with some useful strategies. Private insurance has an important role to play, but an insufficient one. The market cannot produce adequate insurance cover for major long-term risks incurred by whole populations, as Ulrich Beck has pointed out. And it miserably fails to cover poor communities for even minor everyday risks (remember the flooding in Strathclyde where most of the devastated homes were uninsured because the market would not provide that essential cover – it would not take that risk). For these reasons, among others, the market, though useful, can do little to help build a high-trust democracy.

We have considered the need to develop forward-looking strategies for dealing with risk society. What are the main implications for public policy?

A new understanding between public, politicians and experts

First, we need a new deal between the public, the politicians and the experts. A deal to develop and sustain an adult-to-adult relationship. The politicians must learn to act as 'honest broker' between the public and the experts. That means letting the public in on the secrets of the experts, including the very well-guarded secret of the experts' fallibility. It means letting the public in on the limits of the politicians' own knowledge. It also means identifying and publicizing the different interests involved in decisions, and negotiating – openly – between them. That the public have an interest in two capacities, both as citizens and as customers (or users) of goods and services, should be well understood.

We need a new political culture which supports an informed and reasonable scepticism about scientific or expert knowledge. Not Luddite rejection or slavish acquiescence, but somewhere between. That requires clarity and transparency about the interests of the experts – professional or commercial. It requires as much public access as is possible to their knowledge and their deliberations. And public debate about what they say: their ideas, their evidence and their interpretations.

More important still, we need a new political culture which enables politicians to admit they don't have the answer to every question, which enables them to admit they may be wrong, and which applauds rather than ridicules them when they own up to ignorance or change their minds.

More public involvement in decision-making

Second, we need much more public involvement in decision-making, at every level. If the public are treated like children, we may well behave that way. If our only access to policy debates is the tabloid press, we may be forgiven for taking a simplistic view. But if we are passive, apathetic, if we don't turn out to meetings, if we don't vote, it does not follow that we do not deserve democracy. It does not follow that we are useless, passive pawns in the game, who may need protecting but are not worth empowering.

We do have the means to break out of this cycle of passivity and exclusion. At a local level, especially, local authorities and health authorities are creating new forms of dialogue between the public and the decision-makers. There are local public forums and user groups, panels, programmes on radio and television which bring in ordinary members of the public to participate in debates. And citizens' juries, pioneered by the Institute for Public Policy Research in a series of five pilot juries on health-related issues, beginning in March 1996 with the Cambridge and Huntingdon Health Authority.[1]

A citizens' jury involves ordinary members of the public, recruited at random to represent a cross-section of the local community, meeting over a period of four days to address questions of public concern. The first jury, for example, considered health care rationing: what criteria should guide decisions and who should decide. Jurors take evidence from witnesses, cross-examine them, and debate the questions thoroughly before reaching conclusions. They become, in the course of those four days, competent, confident decision-makers, lay experts who feel able to speak for their community. Juries are not a panacea, but they do provide one useful way of encouraging active rather than passive citizenship: informed public participation and effective lay expertise contributing to the policy debate.

Add to this the opportunities offered by new communications technologies. Experiments with electronic democracy, in the US and elsewhere, suggest that more information and more opportunity for participation can be extended to ever greater numbers. Innovations such as these point the way to the kind of open participation which is essential to build a high-trust democracy – treating the public like adults, able and expected to play a full part in decisions. Furthermore, we should not underestimate the enormous importance of education, which, like the mass media, has the potential to increase or diminish active citizenship, depending on how it is organized and delivered.

Planning for uncertainty

Third, we must become skilled at planning for uncertainty. We no longer envisage an ideal end-state to which we are heading. We no longer rely on scientific expertise or economics to predict with any certainty how things will turn out in the future. The further we push out the boundaries of our knowledge, the better able we are to manufacture new uncertainties, and the more we know how impossible it is to be certain about anything.

For example, it is futile to predict how converging communications technologies will affect the way we learn, conduct our relationships, think about ourselves and each other. Or how genetics and biotechnology will change the face of the National Health Service, or the health of the population. Or how either of these developments will influence patterns of social and economic behaviour.

Politicians are notionally responsible for the consequences of human actions over which they have no control – manufactured risks, set in train by science, commerce and technology. Offal is recycled as cattle feed, ozone-depleting gases help keep our food cold, human beings fall in love with the automobile, babies are conceived in test-tubes, satellites bounce signals across the globe ... in all these cases there are no airtight means of predicting or averting risk. As Ulrich Beck has observed, we cannot know what the full effects will be because society itself has become the laboratory and the experiment will run for many years. What can governments do but cross their fingers?

Planning for uncertainty involves, firstly, a clear understanding of the principles that guide policy-making. We may not know the shape of things to come or where we want to end up, but we can decide how we are going to travel, and why. We can be certain, for example, that we want a just distribution of risk and opportunity, that we want to create the conditions for individual autonomy, and for self-help and mutual aid, for enterprise and creativity, for strong relationships and interdependence.

Whatever the policy area, whether it is social justice, media and communications, health policy or family policy, it is important in planning for uncertainty to start with the basics and set out principles before proceeding. This is not about moral absolutes pre-empting politics, but about principles based on a shared set of values providing a framework for decision-making.

Next, we must be clear about what we do know and where we really are at present. Planning for uncertainty involves a realistic appraisal of the evidence at our disposal, a deep understanding of the present (not marred by a rose-tinted view of the past). It involves knowing that we cannot go back. Beck reminds us, referring to Max Weber, that modernization is not a carriage one can step out of at the next corner if one does not like it.

Planning for uncertainty is also about creating laws and institutions which safeguard and promote the principles which are consistent with the evidence and which allow for devolved and flexible decision-making in the future. Enabling where possible, prescribing only when necessary. And decision-making must be open and accountable. Accountability, as John Stewart has pointed out, is not just about periodic elections, but is about a continuing dialogue between the public and the policy-makers. It is a two-way process in which those who are responsible give account and are held to account by those who have vested that responsibility in them.[2]

In risk society, then, public policy requires long-term planning for uncertainty, within a clear framework of principles and evidence to support devolved and flexible decision-making. This in turn requires the involvement of informed and active citizens, enjoying a mature, adult-to-adult relationship both with experts and with politicians. A high-trust democracy: the only way to face a risky future.

Notes

1 A. Coote and J. Lenaghan, *Citizens' Juries: Theory into Practice* (IPPR, London, 1997).
2 J. Stewart, *Innovations in Democratic Practice* (Institute of Local Government Studies, Birmingham, 1995).

Index

accountability 18, 129–30
activism 83–4, 87
Adams, Barbara 17
adaptability 95, 97
Adorno, Theodor 55
AIDS 29–30, 65
air pollution 60–1, 64
alternative medicine 76
Andersen Consulting and
  Nationwide 88
animal growth hormones 58
anthropocentrism 45
anxiety, friendship 110; see also
  insecurity
Arendt, Hannah 15, 113–14
Aristotle 104, 105, 109, 113, 114
asbestos 40–1
asthma 60–1
attachments 92
authoritarianism 126
autonomy 3, 95–6

Bacon, Francis 55
Barings Bank 25
Bauman, Zygmunt 100
Beck, Ulrich: future risk 122–3;
  individualization 26; risk society
  25, 28, 47, 48; society as
  laboratory 9–10, 14, 130

beef crisis 9–10, 24, 43, 44, 47,
  48, 50, 124; see also BSE crisis
Belfast, information technology
  project 88–9
benzene 64
bio-engineering 77
biology 79–80
biotechnology 52, 60–2
Black Report (1984) 59–60
black women, social support 107–8
Blair, Tony 30–1, 101
Bohm, David 78
British Household Panel Study 103,
  117–18 (n7)
British Social Attitudes survey 68,
  103, 117 (n6)
BSE crisis: and CJD 43, 44, 51–2,
  58; costs 33; European conflict
  17; experts 63–4; modernization
  10; need for public dialogue 32;
  precautionary principle 58–9;
  scientists 70, 72–3; see also beef
  crisis
bureaucracy 15

cancer risks 52
candour, in politics 124–5
Capra, Fritjof 55, 78–9
certainty, need for 125

CFCs 57
Chernobyl plant 28–9, 43
Chiba, Shin 114
childhood, relationships 92–3, 97
choice expansion 30
citizens' juries 128–9
citizenship 100
Clarke, Arthur C. 81
class 25, 30, 33, 109, 110
climatic disturbances 24–5, 39,
    54–5, 66, 67
Committee for the Scientific
    Investigation of Claims of the
    Paranormal 76, 79, 80
Commission on Social Justice 88–9
commitment 101
communication 105, 107, 108
community, idealized 2–3, 90, 100
consciousness studies 80
consumerism 24, 77
contentment 99
convergence 84, 87–8
corruption 25
cover-ups 29
Creutzfeldt-Jakob disease 43, 45,
    59
critical theory 55
culture: and nature 10–11; and
    science 77

Dawkins, Richard 79
decision-making, public involvement
    128
Deering, Michael 81
definition, relations of 18
democracy: electronic 129; high-
    trust 7, 126, 131; technical 21
dependency 95–6, 101, 102, 123
deregulation 44
destabilizing effect, convergence 84
Dorrell, Stephen 124
Drinking Water Directive 58

e-mail 84
ecological crises 16
ecology 33, 55
Einstein, Albert 78
electronic democracy 129
emotional dependency 95–6, 101,
    102

emotional literacy 97–8
Enlightenment project 54, 55–6, 76
enterprise culture, contentment 99
environment: and consumerism 77;
    degradation 18; human impact
    29; pollution regulation 63
Environment Agency 63
environmental movement 71
environmental risks 54–6, 68
Etzioni, A. 99
eukaryotic cells 79
European Union: BSE crisis 17;
    Drinking Water Directive 58;
    Maastricht Treaty 56
evolutionary biology 79
Ewald, François 11, 20
experts: and politicians 63–4;
    psychotherapists 96; and public
    125; reliance on 50–1; risk
    advisers 1, 5; scientists 5,
    13–14, 50–1, 70–1

family: deficiencies 99; and
    friendship 103, 104–6; gender
    32–3, 102; as model for political
    relations 112; relationships 6–7,
    91–2; stability 6–7; structure
    102
farming, industrialized 45, 46
feminism 97
Feynman, Richard 79
food industry 33, 57–8
food stocks, global 61
fragmentation 16, 99–100
Frankfurt School 55
fraud 36, 40
Friends of the Earth 57
friendship: communication 105,
    107, 108; deinstitutional 112–13;
    equality 109, 110; and family
    103, 104–6; and happiness
    103–4; identity 114–15; politics
    108–9, 111, 113; Self and Other
    109–10; social 104, 105, 107–8;
    social cohesion 6–7; as
    subversive 106–7, 108–9
futures markets 25

Gaia 80
Galbraith, J. K. 33

gender, emotional dependency
95–6, 101, 102
genetic determinism 79
genetic engineering 46, 61, 62
genetically modified organisms 52
Giddens, Anthony: modernization
48; relationships 102; socialism/
conservatism 9
global capital 84–5
global food stocks 61
global warming 4, 24, 64–7
Goodwin, Brian 79–80
government: *see* politicians; politics
green politics 120–1
greenhouse effect 65
growth hormones 57–8

happiness 103–4
Harappa culture 54
Hastings, Max 36
Hawking, Stephen 82
hazard 19, 26–7
health care 20
HIV 65
Horkheimer, Max 55
human community 90
human impact 11, 29, 43–4
human subject 91
Hutter, H. 108, 110
hybrid world 11

Icelandic society 54–5
identity, friendship 114–15
impact, and knowledge 17, 19–20
The Independent 9
individualization 26
industrialization 45, 46
information technology: Belfast
project 88–9; economic divisions
88; empowering 86; networks
5, 83–4; relationships 86–7
insecurity 2, 85, 90, 126
Institute for Public Policy Research
128–9
institutions 31, 53
insurance cycle 38–9
insurance industry: compensation
16; economic costs 127; fraud
36, 40; global warming 67;
private 27; public 27; risk

assessment 12, 67; risk spreading
35, 37; taxation 41; uninsurability
121; welfare state 20; *see also*
Lloyd's insurance market
interactive media kiosk 88
Intergovernmental Panel on Climate
Change 64, 65
Internet, political activism 83–4,
87
irresponsibility, organized 15, 18

Jordan, A. 56

Kauffman, Stuart 81
knowledge: and impact 17, 19–20;
scientific 23–4, 31–2; status 71;
technical 11
knowledge capital 84
knowledge workers 85
Kurtz, Paul 76

Latour, Bruno 11, 19
lead pollution 64–5
Leason, Nick 25
legitimacy of politics 4
leukaemia clusters 59–60
liability, unlimited 36, 41–2
lifestyle politics 33
Lloyd's insurance market: annual
trading venture 40; entry
standards 38; incompetence 39;
losses 37–9; names 35–7, 40;
risk changes 3, 24–5; risk/
reward ratio 41; underwriters
35, 37
LMX spiral 38–9
Lovelock, James 80

Maastricht Treaty 56
magic and science 81
male fertility levels 24, 45, 52
management, new technology 86
Margulis, Lynn 79–80
market, risk 126–7
medicine 57, 76
modernity: deference to science 71;
first to second phase 2;
government 123; radicalized 20;
reflexivity 17–18, 20–1, 107;
technical knowledge 11

modernization: institutions 31;
　political 48; reflexive 31, 33–4;
　risk-generating 10; simple 31
Moore, Gordon 84
moral commitments 101
morality 108
mysticism 76, 79

natural disasters 66; *see also*
　climatic disturbances
nature: and culture 10–11; human
　impact 43–4; and human species
　45; and risk society 3, 5, 10, 26,
　28; science 55; taming of 55,
　56; and technology 3
neo-Darwinism 79
neoliberalism, profits/public safety 44
networks 5–6, 83–4
New Age, new scientific paradigm
　81
New Labour 30–1, 126
New Right 44, 123
New Statesman 37
NORL General Social Survey (1985)
　104
nostalgia 6
nuclear weapons 71, 78

object relationships 94
organizations, control 85; *see also*
　institutions
O'Riordan, T. 56
ozone layer 57, 66

Panglossian principle 59–60
partners 105–6
paternalism 111
Penrose, Roger 80
pensions 121
pesticides 57–8, 60
petrol, superunleaded 64
physics 78–9
political activism 83–4, 87
politicians: accountability 129–30;
　and experts 63–4; as honest
　broker 127–8; and public
　125–6; and scientists 52
politics: candour 124–5;
　convergence 87–8; friendship
　108–9, 111, 113; legitimacy 4;

lifestyle 33; nostalgia 6;
　propitiation 47; purges 108–9;
　risk management 1, 29, 49, 122,
　123; risk society 1, 2–3, 6, 7–8;
　special interest groups 32, 34;
　state shedding 122; technology
　14–15, 89; voters 111–12
pollution: air 60, 64; lead 64;
　pay/prove principle 21; regulation
　63; reinsurance 40–1
Popper, Karl 14, 23
postmodernism 33–4, 72, 74
Powell, Enoch 32
precautionary principle 4, 56–9, 62
prediction 120–1
Prigogine, Ilya 80
procrastination 63–9
production relations 18
profits/public safety 44
propitiation 47
psychoanalysis 91
psychotherapist, as expert 96
public, and politicians 125–6
public debate 128
Public Health Laboratory 67
public health threats 43–5, 51
public opinion 68–9, 72, 74
public policy 5, 7–8, 57–8, 125
purges, political 108–9

quantum physics 78
quasi-objects 19

rationality 77–8
reflexivity 17–18, 20–1, 31, 33–4,
　107
reinsurance 39, 40–1
relations of definition/production
　18
relationship types: confluent 102;
　enabling 94, 96; family 6–7,
　91–2; internal 93–4; object
　relationship 94; sexual 105–6;
　social 101–2
relationships: autonomy 3, 95–6;
　emotional dependency 95–6;
　information technology 86–7;
　loyalty 86–7; psychoanalysis 91;
　responsibilities 106; in risk
　society 94–5; social cohesion 6–7

reproductive technology 30
responsibility 15, 18–19, 129–30
risk 1, 3; consumers 24; and
future 27, 122–3; and hazard
26–7; and insurance 12, 35, 37,
67; market 126–7; opacity 39;
proof 59–61; public policy 5,
7–8; responsibility for 15; takers/
victims 10
risk, types: boundary crossing
16–17; calculated 60–2;
environmental 54–6, 68; for
excitement 12; external 27–8;
global 17–18; manufactured 28,
32–3, 48–9, 54
risk assessment 12, 66–7, 73–4
risk innovation 52–3
risk management 62–3;
authoritarianism 126; backward-
looking strategy 126–7;
economic considerations 63;
insurance 35, 37; politics 1, 29,
49, 122, 123; precautionary
principle 62; prediction 120,
121–2
risk society: individuals 1, 2; as
laboratory 9–10, 130; and nature
3, 5, 10, 26, 28; New Labour
30–1; opportunities 21; origins
122; politics 1, 2–3, 6, 7–8; as
radicalized modernity 20;
rationality 77–8; relationships
94–5; residual 17; responsibility
18–19; science 47, 48; and
tradition 3, 5, 10, 26
Rose, Hilary 16
Ross, Andrew 80–1
Royal Commission on
Environmental Pollution 61
Royal Society, *Risk Analysis* 62

Sagan, Carl 78
Samuels, Andrew 96
scaremongering 29, 30
scepticism 4, 72
science: BSE 70, 72–3; everyday life
23; as expert adviser 5, 13–14,
50–1, 70–1; and knowledge
23–4, 31–2; and magic 81; and
nature 55; new paradigm 5,
80–1; objectivity 78–9;
Panglossian principle 59–60;
politicians 52; precautionary
principle 56–7; public opinion
72, 74, 77; risk assessment
73–4; risk society 47, 48;
scepticism towards 72, 77
scientific research 51
Sebag Montefiore, Simon 25, 31
security 2, 95
self-regard 93
Sellafield, leukaemia clusters 59
Shiva, Vandana 55–6
Silver, Allan 106–7
social anthropologists 115
social cohesion 6–7, 99, 101
social distance 109
socialism 9, 100, 101, 111
society: fragmented 16, 99–100;
as laboratory 9–10, 14, 130;
networks 84; relationships 6–7,
91–2; and science 77; security
2; support mechanisms 107–8
sociologists 115
solidarity 100–1, 111
special interest groups 32, 34
Spectator 36
sperm counts 24, 45, 52
Stack, Carol 107
state shedding 122
stepfamilies 102
sub-atomic physics 78
subjectivity 91
subpoliticization 16
subversion by friendship 106–7,
108–9
support systems, social 107–8

taxation 41
technical democracy 21
technology: choice 30; and nature
3; outer edge 25; politics
14–15, 89; reproductive 30
Technology Foresight Programme
63
telekinesis 81
telepathy 81
thought-controlled interfaces 81
tomatoes, genetically modified 62
tradition, risk society 3, 5, 10, 26

trust   7, 109, 116, 126
2,4,5-T pesticide   59–60

uncertainty: manufactured   12–13;
   planning for   129–31;
   procrastination   63–9; shared
   53
uninsurability   121
US, Super Fund reforms   41
utopia, active   100

values   8
Varela, Francisco   80

virtual reality   81
voters   111–12

water quality   57–8
welfare state   15–16, 20, 27–8,
   32–3, 121
Willmott, Peter   103
wine, health benefits   24
work control   85–6
work team, virtual   86
World Health Organisation   64

Zeldin, T.   102